SEX

with a
Cheater, Abuser, Addict

Written by
Dee (Pepper) Lois

authorHOUSE®

AuthorHouse™
1663 Liberty Drive
Bloomington, IN 47403
www.authorhouse.com
Phone: 1-800-839-8640

First published by AuthorHouse 1/25/2010

ISBN: 978-1-4490-3732-1 (e)
ISBN: 978-1-4490-3730-7 (sc)
ISBN: 978-1-4490-3731-4 (hc)

Library of Congress Control Number: 2009913955

Printed in the United States of America
Bloomington, Indiana

This book is printed on acid-free paper.

Chapter 1

I'M WRITING THIS letter to all my sisters around the world who have been verbally abused by a man. I know exactly what you're going through. For years I was constantly forced to deal with my man's ostracism and indifference. I was trapped in a world where mental abuse reigned supreme. His influence over me was paralyzing. There was no room for me to grow, to live or to simply be. He was enveloping my whole life. He was smothering me. It wasn't just my mental abuse that I was concerned with, but that of my children as well. Ladies, hearing mommy being verbally abused over and over again is child abuse. I had even contemplated committing suicide. My husband wasn't interested in working to establish peace and harmony in our relationship. His behavior was totally inappropriate. We had become a dysfunctional family where my husband was constantly subjecting me and the children to verbal and emotional abuse. He was happy with turmoil and chaos. Your man may be behaving the same way. Ladies, it's not your fault. The psychosocial impact that abuse has made on our society has become detrimental to us all. It is destroying families. It is destroying lives. It is destroying the mental and emotional growth of our children. Abuse has become more and more prevalent in all walks of life. It doesn't matter if you are rich, poor or a celebrity. Abuse affects us all. Domestic violence is growing globally in unprecedented severity and quantity. Women are dying at the hands of the men that are supposed to love them. I did what a lot of abused women do. I was actually enabling my man to be an abuser.

I thought to myself, "He's a good man. He would never put his hands on me. He would never slap me or punch me or send me to the hospital with bruises and broken bones."

Yes, he called me a slut and a stupid bitch. He told me that I was fat and that if I ever left him that no other man would want me. He told me on more than one occasion that I was a worthless piece of shit. He told me that I couldn't cook, clean, make love right and that I was one of the worst mothers he had ever seen. But, he never beat me. That's something, isn't it? The uncertainty of the continuation of our relationship tormented me. I couldn't sleep at night and couldn't rest during the day. I became a nervous wreck. I stopped living. I stopped being. I just ate and ate whenever I had the chance. Food became my comforter. My sedentary lifestyle and poor eating habits led to my obesity. I began to feel as though my obesity was a contributing factor in the breakdown of our relationship. It was my fault. I allowed myself to become unattractive and fat. I couldn't face myself in the mirror. I was ashamed of my appearance and of whom I had become. My husband had a right to treat me the way he did. Right? The truth of the matter was that even if I were a size two he would still be mentally and verbally abusing me. But it was my fault. I wasn't a good wife. I did use food as escapism from his verbal and mental abuse. But, during all that, he was man enough never to lay a hand on me.

I thought, "He deserves credit for that. Right? He didn't hit me because he loved me. He's not an abusive man." Am I right ladies?

Ladies please do not be my judge and jury. I am not the only one. There are millions of women all around the world just like me. We are one in the same. For a long time I was a bundle of nerves at all times. I tried to live a low-profile life so that I could hide my shame. I couldn't hide the hurt and humiliation I faced each and every day. Family and friends could see it. They were all concerned for me and the kids. I felt uneasiness every time he woke up in the morning, when he went to bed with me at night, the few occasions that we made love and even when he came home from work. It wasn't the bundle of nerves that a woman feels when she is in love and her man is coming to be with her. It was the bundle of nerves you feel when you just know something bad is about to happen and that bad thing was just going to keep happening over and over again. For a long time I was in a chronic state of depression. The unrelenting verbal abuse wore me down. I prayed at night for God to deliver me from the torment that I was held prisoner in. My prayers were never answered, or so I thought. What I didn't realize was that God had already released me from the ties that bound me. All I needed to do was ask for help from my family, friends or the authorities. I only needed to believe in a mighty God. I realize that for many women all over the world with men that are enraged and dangerous that sometimes it is not as easy as that and that their lives are in danger. I was luckier. My husband wasn't the physically violent man. He was mentally abusive. My life and that of my children was never really in danger. It was easier for me to leave. For those women whose lives are in danger, they definitely need professional help. They may not be able to escape without help. The stress that he caused me had a direct physiologic affect on my health. Physical and mental abuse of any kind can have a detrimental effect on our health. I became profoundly fatigued and had a total lack of energy. My heart ached and I felt anxious all the time. It was like going through emotional starvation. Then I woke up. I realized that he wasn't willing to accept any responsibility for the destruction of our relationship. He blamed everything on me and I told myself he was right. I stopped doing that.

I thought to myself, "What are you talking about? This jerk has the nerve to call me worthless and that I am one of the worst mothers he has ever seen. Who does he think he is?"

What about my daughter ladies? She was growing up listening to her daddy call her mommy a fat bitch and a worthless piece of shit. How was that affecting her? Would she too grow up and allow men to physically and mentally abuse her? What kind of teenager would she become? I've seen parents struggle with their teenaged daughters. Peer pressure is hard and these are trying times that we are living in today. The pressures that teens have to deal with are immense. They have to deal with drugs, gangs, exaggerated body images with skinny models and unrealistic television ads, increased violence in our society, recessions, homelessness and more. Would my daughter grow up to believe that her outward appearance is much more important than the woman she is inside? My daughter was growing up too fast. Listening to all the verbal abuse going on in her world was maturing her at a rapid pace even though she was still my little girl. She wasn't being allowed the joy of just being a little girl. She was only at the ripe age of five and was already beginning to ask if she was getting too fat. She was urinating in her bed at night and was having difficulty sleeping. I was her mother and I was failing her. How could I properly take care of her if I was incapable of taking care of myself? What kind of woman would she become?

I became fed up. I deserved better than this. My children definitely deserved better than this. I told myself I will never allow anyone, male or female, to disrespect me and talk to me the way this man did. I took care of my children all of these years the best way I knew how and I was able to give them the better part of my personality despite my husband. I gave them the ability to love, to respect life, to learn, to grow and to explore. What I didn't give them until now was the ability to respect themselves enough to not let anyone verbally abuse them. They grew up listening to daddy call mommy a slut, a stupid bitch, and a worthless piece of garbage. This is something that I will spend the rest of my life correcting. But the first thing I had to do was get rid of Kenneth. The bastard had to go. I dug deep within my soul and realized that my God in Heaven didn't want me to be treated like this. I exclaimed to my man that I couldn't take his abuse any longer and that he had to get out of not only my life but that of our kids as well. God wanted me to be respected as a woman and as his daughter. Ladies think back to the time in your life when you were full of faith in Jesus and you felt truly blessed by him. You read your bible religiously. You attended church regularly. You prayed at night before you went to bed for God to protect you and your loved ones and to guide you the next morning. You lifted your hands up in the morning to glorify the Lord. Then you met your man and because of years of abuse you forgot that you were the daughters of a mighty God.

Maybe you felt abandoned by God. Maybe the very essence of who you were has been crushed so low that you don't have the emotional or spiritual strength to pick up your bible and pray. God never abandoned you. He saw every slap, punch, and kick you endured. God saw every time he cheated on you with other women. He heard every time your man verbally and physically abused you. He saw your tears, felt your pain and heard your cries. God knew. One day your man will have to stand before a mighty God in the final judgment and he has a lot of explaining to do. God wants you to come back to him. Trust in him again. Pick up your bible again and pray. Ask Jesus for forgiveness and allow the Holy Spirit of God to come into your life again and give you guidance. Become spiritually revitalized. Allow a mighty God to put your spirit at peace. Trust in him again. He has always loved you and no matter what has happened or what you have to go through he always will. For a long time I blamed myself for everything that was wrong in our relationship. I tried everything I could to please Kenneth, but he never seemed to be satisfied. I began to feel encumbered by his constant nagging and verbal abuse. My spirit was brought very low. I lost my self-esteem. I was not a good enough wife for him. He wanted more. But, more of what? I don't think even Kenneth knew what he wanted. I realize now that I wasn't the problem. Kenneth was the problem. He was a verbally abusive man. His verbal and mental abuse destroyed our relationship. It wasn't my fault.

Ladies, please do not judge me for staying with him this long and tolerating his verbal and mental abuse. I am not alone. There are millions of women like me all over the world. They are being mentally and verbally abused right at this moment. We are the same. We are as one.

———•———

Kenneth woke up and went into the bathroom to take a shower. He forgot to bring a towel into the bathroom so he yelled for me to bring him one.

I brought the towel to him and he yelled, "What the fuck is the matter with you Teresa? You know damn well I have to take a shower in the mornings. Why can't you have a towel waiting for me like other wives do? You're such a worthless piece of fat shit!"

It didn't take much to trigger his anger. His bursts of anger appeared suddenly and progressed quickly into total rage. He wasn't always like this. When we first got married he treated me like a queen. He was sweet and kind and talked to me with the utmost respect. As time went on he changed. The change was subtle and overlooked by me. I didn't realize that it would get this bad. Whenever I expressed opposition to his dominant behavior the abuse and insults worsened. There had been gentleness to his soul that made me fall in love with him in the first place. That gentleness was gone. He was now as cold as ice. He snatched the towel out of my hands. I walked out of the bathroom and went into the kitchen to prepare breakfast for the family. This is how he talked to me. We rarely made love and when we did I trembled in revulsion at his touch. My family and I lived in Boston, Massachusetts. I was a thirty-seven year old housewife and mother of three children. I had a five year old daughter, an eight year old son and a ten year old son. My children were growing up listening to their father verbally abusing me over and over again. What was this doing to my daughter's self-esteem and self-worth? What was this doing to my sons and their attitude toward women? Even though I asked myself these questions over and over again I still stayed with Kenneth and put up with years of his bullshit. He scolded me constantly as though I was his child and he was raising me. He stopped treating me like a woman, like a grown-up. I fell right into the mold. I allowed him to act as my father and I as his daughter, even though I was his wife.

The kids came downstairs one at a time and sat at the kitchen table. I fed them breakfast and fixed a plate for Kenneth. I didn't want him to have to wait for one second for a plate because then I would have to hear his big mouth and I wasn't in the mood to listen to him bitch and complain. Kenneth came downstairs a few minutes later and sat down to breakfast.

He took one bite of the eggs and said nastily, "The eggs are cold Teresa. This is how you serve breakfast to someone? What the fuck is the matter with you? Are you stupid or something? Heat the damn breakfast Teresa."

I took his plate and put it in the microwave. I heated his food and then gave it back to him.

My eight and ten year old sons said, "Mom our breakfasts are cold too. Heat them up. Heat them up now!" They were sounding more and more like their father. I took their plates and warmed them in the microwave. I was afraid to scold them out of fear of what my husband would have to say about it. This would have been the opportune moment for him to call me a lousy mother.

Next, my five year old daughter yelled, "Teresa heat the damn breakfast. Mommy is such a worthless piece of shit."

My husband screamed at her and said, "Hey! You want me to wash your mouth out with soap?"

"No daddy."

"Ok, that's enough," he said angrily. "Everybody get up and get ready for school. I'm dropping you off today." My kids got up and got ready for their dad to take them to school.

"You think that since I'm taking the kids to school you can get up off your lazy ass and clean up this house? This place looks like a pig's pen. All you do is sit around on your ass all day long and nothing gets done. You have the whole damn day to get this place clean and it's still dirty. You are such a worthless piece of shit."

My five year old daughter marched around the house like a soldier. She repeated over and over again, "Mommy is a worthless piece of shit. Mommy is a worthless piece of shit."

My husband yelled out to my ten-year-old son, "Dammit Billy, take your little sister and brother to the car and stay with them until I get there."

"Ok dad," he responded. He took his brother and sister to the car.

After the kids had gone outside I asked, "Why do you have to be so ugly Kenneth? Why do you have to talk to me like that around the kids? You can see how it's affecting them. The boys are already starting to disrespect their little sister and they talk down to her as though she's beneath them. And Tina, she's cursing constantly. She sounds like a sailor."

Kenneth became furious. He screamed, "Who the fuck do you think you are? You gonna tell me what I can and can't say in my own home? Who pays the bills around here? I know your lazy ass doesn't. Let me tell you something. I'm the man in this house and I'll say whatever the fuck I want to. The kids are the way they are because of your stupid ass. You're too soft with them. You let them get away with everything and now you want to blame me because you're such a lousy mother. You know what? I don't have time for this. Wasting my time with your lazy ass is gonna make me late for work. Get out of my face you stupid bitch."

He grabbed his tools and lunch box and stormed out the door. He slammed the front door so hard I thought it was going to fall right off of its hinges. I started to clean up the house as my husband had ordered me to. After all, he was the man of the house as he so eloquently put it. This was my life with Kenneth each and every day. He wakes up in the morning whining, complaining and verbally assaulting me and goes to bed every evening doing the same thing. Sometimes I wonder if he loves me at all.

"It's not his fault though. I do need to become a better wife and mother. This house really is a mess. I really do need to make some improvements. If I do things better Kenneth won't get so mad at me. It's really all my fault. I really am too fat." These are the things I told myself for years.

I trivialized my own suffering and his abuse. I debated with myself many times over the years on whether I should leave him. Then I talked myself out of it and convinced myself that all of our marital problems were my fault. It wasn't an easy decision to make. The answer to whether or not to leave would not only affect my life but that of our kids as well. What about them? On one hand, staying with my husband and allowing him to constantly belittle and verbally abuse me was damaging to our kids but, on the other hand leaving him would also destroy our children mentally. I was torn. I didn't know what to do. How could I separate them from their daddy and rip the family apart? How could I stay and put up with his abuse? I convinced myself that I had to sacrifice myself for my children and stay with my husband even if he abused me. I didn't want to hurt my children so I stayed. I stayed and endured the pain and humiliation of his abuse in private and in public.

It got to the point where Kenneth didn't even try to hide the abuse. He verbally insulted me right in front of others. Let me give you ladies an example. Kenneth and I decided to have a dinner party one Sunday night. It was the Super Bowl weekend and football was on everybody's mind. It was east coast vs. west coast and excitement filled the air. Football parties were being given all over the city. We had invited several of our closest friends over for dinner, drinks and laughs. I prepared the entire dinner myself. The kids stayed over their grandparent's house for the weekend, which was a big load off of me. I could really get things done. Everything was almost ready by the time Kenneth got home. He arrived home around four that afternoon. He was excited about getting together with his buddies. Whenever they got together they would drink, talk about sports, cars, sex and women and act a total fool.

Kenneth burst into the kitchen and asked, "Is everything ready? Everybody will be here soon."

"Not quite. Everything is almost ready. Don't worry. I'll have everything done on time."

"Got dammit Teresa!" he yelled. "You are so slow. You've been here all day long and you still don't have your shit together? What were you doing all day long? Were you just sitting on your fat ass watching soap operas and eating ice cream? Take your thumb out of your ass and get moving. I want everything perfect by the time the guests get here. Don't fuck up!"

"Kenneth, why are you yelling at me like that? That's not even called for. I said everything is almost ready. By the time the guests arrive everything will be done. Don't worry."

"When it comes to you I have to worry because you always fuck everything up," he responded nastily. As he headed upstairs to get dressed, he yelled out, "Did you take my brown shirt out like I asked you to?"

"Kenneth you told me that you were wearing your blue shirt tonight. That's the shirt I took out. It's hanging on the back of the bedroom door."

"Damn it Teresa," he yelled out. "What is the matter with you? Do you have peanuts for a brain? I said I wanted to wear the brown fucking shirt tonight. You know, you have to be the stupidest bitch I've ever been with. I don't even know why I married your dumb ass. I should have married your younger sister. She's the smart one of all your siblings and boy is she pretty. And what a sweet ass she has."

I just ignored Kenneth and continued what I was doing. After Kenneth finished dressing he came back downstairs. I don't even know why he was bitching. He had on the same blue shirt that I had taken out. Everything was finally ready and I began to set the dining room table.

Kenneth came up behind me, picked up one of the wine glasses and said, "These glasses are not clean Teresa."

"Kenneth I just took these out of the dishwasher. They're all clean."

"I'm sitting here looking at water spots all over these glasses Teresa. So obviously they're not clean enough. Am I right? Take your thumb out of your ass and wash the fucking glasses again. Do it now Teresa."

I started picking up the glasses so that I could put them back in the dishwasher as Kenneth had ordered.

"And don't put them back in the dishwasher," he demanded. "I want you to hand wash each and every one of them. I want them done right this time."

I wanted to tell him to hand wash them himself and then take each and every last one of them and shove them up his ass, but I didn't. I didn't want to piss him off any more than he already was right before the guests were due to arrive. I just did as he asked. Finally everything was ready. I had already gotten myself dressed so all I needed to do was wait for Kenneth to come back downstairs.

He finally came back downstairs and asked, "Is that what you're gonna wear?"

"Yes Kenneth. This is my favorite dress."

"The reason why you always look like shit is because you're so fat. You need to lose some weight Teresa. When I first married you, you were so skinny. Now look at you. You look like a fat cow."

"What's the matter with you Kenneth?" I asked. "Why do you have to be so nasty right before the party? You don't have to talk to me like that. I'm not skinny like I was when we first got married because I'm getting older and I did have three children. In fact, they're your three children Kenneth. You had a part in getting me pregnant or don't you remember?"

"A lot of women have children and they figure out a way to lose the fat Teresa. Your problem is not that you've had three children. Your problem is that you eat too much. You're always stuffing your mouth with something. If you closed your big mouth and stopped stuffing it with food Teresa you wouldn't be so fat. Every time you open your mouth you're stuffing something in it. Maybe if I put my foot in your mouth and shoved it all the way down your throat you wouldn't have time to put food in it."

Kenneth was really starting to get on my nerves. Thank god the guests finally started to arrive because I really got tired of listening to him insulting me.

One by one the guests arrived and we greeted them at the door. They each had wine, dessert or flowers as gifts. I accepted them all gracefully. The ladies congregated into the living room to talk and gossip. The men made their way to the den to watch football on the television. Kenneth was the life of the party as usual. He was able to engage everyone with his wit and humor. Believe it or not ladies when he wanted to, he could be very funny. He just refused to do it with me. He was beaming with charisma. His charisma lasted for about five minutes.

"Hey Teresa bring some beer in here for me and the guys."

I excused myself from the other ladies and went to the kitchen to get the guys some cold beer.

"What's taking you so long? Hurry up and move your fat ass."

"Here Kenneth. Calm down. I heard you the first time."

The other ladies began to whisper amongst each other. They were surprised at how ignorant my husband was acting. This was a side of him that none of them had ever seen before. I on the other hand, had seen it and knew it all too well. I was terrified of this side of him. I hated this side of him.

I gave him several cans of ice cold beer and went back to join the ladies. Later we adjourned to the dining area for dinner. There was great food and great conversation. Only I felt excluded from the conversations that were taking place. My husband took over each conversation and when I tried to join in he interrupted me as though I didn't know what I was talking about.

He would say things like, "What you are saying doesn't make sense or why don't you wait and talk when you know what you're talking about because you are making a fool out of yourself."

He was making a complete spectacle of himself. My friends began to feel a little uneasy and were embarrassed for me. It was humiliating. My husband was doing what he did best. He was disrespecting and ignoring me again. His hatred of me had become indubitable. He wasn't trying to hide his feelings anymore. It was as though he wanted everyone to know how much he hated and abhorred me. I had become an inconvenience to him. My husband laughed at me hysterically right in front of everyone. His lack of love and respect had become indisputable. The dinner party was a success to my husband but for me and the other guests it was a total disaster. We all said goodbye and everyone went home. I guess you realize that was the last time any of them ever showed up at my house again. I went into the kitchen and cleaned everything up. Kenneth went to the den to unwind and watch television. After I finished I went into the den to join my husband.

I sat down on the couch next to him and asked, "Why are you so angry with me? Don't you want to make our marriage work? Let's just forget about the evening and just start over. I love you and I want us to work."

My husband just ignored me.

"You know it's been a long time since we've made love together. Everyone's gone. The kids are at their grandparent's house. This is the perfect time for us to be together. You want to fool around? I would love to be with you tonight."

Kenneth looked at me with a disapproving look. "The reason why we don't make love together anymore is because you don't take care of yourself," he said with disgust. "I'm not attracted to you anymore. Look how fat you are. You don't even take pride in yourself. Why would I want to make love to a fat woman like you? You're fat, ugly and I'm not turned on by you anymore. You don't do it for me anymore baby," he said as he laughed hysterically in my face.

I searched his face to see a sign, any sign of love. All I could see and feel from him was his hate and disgust with me. I groped and searched for just a little bit of compassion from him. He had none to give me. He gave me loathe. The love and attention that I requested from him was reasonable. I asked nothing out of the ordinary. I asked for an occasional kiss, an occasional touch or an occasional box of chocolate. I got absolutely nothing from him. Even at Christmas time I would buy myself a gift, a small trinket, just to say I had received something. I would wrap it myself and put it underneath the Christmas tree for all to see what my husband supposedly had bought me. Nobody suspected that he had bought me nothing. My husband came from humble beginnings and his family's dysfunctional background shaped who he was today. If he would have utilized his energy to build up our relationship instead of ripping it apart with his abuse, our family would not have been destroyed. Tears rolled down my cheeks. I tried to hold them back but was unsuccessful. At that moment even if he did touch me I would have become repulsed. I was beginning to awaken from the illusion that my husband actually loved me.

"You know what, forget it. I'm going to bed. I'm not going to sit here and let you insult me like this." I got up and went upstairs to bed alone again. Kenneth never joined me and in fact, he fell asleep on the couch that night.

Kenneth was not only verbally abusive around friends, but family as well. He was becoming more and more temperamental and mean. I remember one day we took the kids over to his parent's house for a family barbeque. His entire family was there including his nephews and nieces, his three brothers and their wives, a couple of cousins and of course, his parents. We were all out back in the backyard enjoying the afternoon. You could smell barbeque everywhere. The kids were all running around playing games. The ladies were all preparing the food. The guys were in charge of barbecuing and drinking beer. I was starving so I fixed myself a few spoons of potato salad just to get a taste.

Kenneth saw me eating and he yelled out, "Yeah, there you go doing your favorite pastime, stuffing your mouth like a fat pig. You can't even wait for the rest of us. Damn Teresa!"

"Hush Kenneth," his mom pleaded. She was very embarrassed for me. "You don't talk to your wife like that. Not around me you don't."

"Look at her," Kenneth said nastily. "Look how fat she's gotten. You remember how skinny she was when we first got married man. I guess those days are over, huh Teresa?"

I was so embarrassed. I wanted to hide my face so no one could see me. I couldn't hide my shame. Everyone was looking at me at this time.

His brother Lucas said, "You had too much to drink Kenneth. You need to calm down. You're embarrassing your wife. Stop it."

"Ok, ok. I'm sorry. I'm sorry. I was just fucking around with Teresa." He said sarcastically, "You know I love you baby." He started laughing out loud. In his attempt at embarrassing me, he made a complete spectacle of himself in front of his family. At that moment they were all ashamed of him.

I ran inside the house to hide. I couldn't face his family. His sister-in-law Becky came into the house to comfort me. "He just had a little too much to drink," she said. "He loves you honey." I held my head down in shame. I couldn't tell her that my own husband abhorred and hated me. Kenneth continued to verbally abuse me like this for years and I just tolerated it. I had such a low self esteem that I didn't even realize that I could do better than Kenneth. I started to believe that I really was a fat worthless piece of shit as Kenneth frequently called me.

After several weeks had passed he decided that he wanted to make love to me. I was already in bed when he came into the bedroom. He took his clothes off and climbed into bed with me. He reached for me and I scooted over to him. I was feeling very lonely at that time and I needed my husband to forget about abusing me for one moment and make me feel like a woman for once. He kissed me and then caressed my breasts. As his manhood grew I was getting really turned on and it felt like he was too. He reached down and rubbed his hands over my legs. He suddenly stopped. He couldn't even make love to me without verbally abusing me.

"Damn Teresa. Your breath stinks so bad it's making me nauseous. Don't you ever shave your legs? It feels like I'm rubbing against a brush. Your stomach feels bigger than it ever has before. You can't be pregnant because I haven't touched your fat ass in awhile and I know no other man wants to touch you. You must be eating too fucking much food. You need to lose weight. I feel like I'm making love to a fucking whale."

I couldn't believe that even during intimacy he couldn't resist verbally abusing me. I tried to push him off of me. I refused to make love to him at that moment. He became furious.

"Oh so you're going to act like that? You're going to turn into a bitch now? Fuck you then! You're too disgusting for a man to touch anyway. Who needs you? Who fucking wants you? Bitch!"

As he climbed off of me he pushed me aside like I was nothing. He turned over and went to sleep. I hid my face as I cried myself to sleep.

Believe it or not things became even more unbearable for me. My husband's abuse worsened and our family was headed toward total collapse. Our relationship became completely stagnant. We didn't make love anymore and there were no more kind moments left for me to enjoy. Kenneth not only was verbally abusing me in front of the kids, but he also started encouraging them to join in. It was as though he had no conscience.

He would say things like, "Teresa the food is not cooked right. Hey kids don't you think that your mom needs to take some cooking lessons? Teresa you are getting too fat. Look at yourself in the mirror. You look like a pig. Hey kids, don't you think your mom looks like a pig? Oink! Oink!"

My sons who were at this time eleven and thirteen now would pick on their little sister who was now eight and call her a worthless piece of shit. My daughter was cursing more and more as time went on and she was even doing it at school. I received many phone calls and had to make multiple visits to her school about her foul mouth. My husband's mood swings were also becoming more and more unpredictable. I was on edge all of the time. His constant criticism beat me down emotionally. I couldn't sleep at night because of increased anxiety and insomnia. I felt more and more isolated and distanced from him. We were no longer a couple. We weren't really even husband and wife anymore. We were like strangers living together under one roof just to torment and hurt one another. It was like being locked up with your worst enemy.

Finally I had enough. One day I stood in front of a full length mirror. I was completed naked. I looked at my reflection in the mirror and said out loud, "You are a beautiful woman. You are worth something. You are special and no man has the right to treat you like this. Why are you tolerating this abuse from this asshole? He is not worth it? He is not worth having you? You are not the pathetic piece of shit that he has called you all of these years. He is. He is not worth having you. He is not worth having any woman. Your kids need you. Your kids need you to stand up and show them who their mother really is. They need to see just what a phenomenal woman you are. Your children are being mentally and spiritually abused right with you. Do something to save those beautiful growing children. Do something before he destroys the very essence of who they are inside."

I realized that I liked myself. I liked being a mom. I liked being a woman. Hell, I survived years of verbal and mental abuse from a jackass man like my husband. That was proof that I was strong. I did have what it would take to raise my children on my own. I was stronger than I could ever imagine. I was a phenomenal woman. I even liked the woman that I had become in spite of the abuse that I received from my husband. I decided at the moment that I had to not only get myself away from this man, but my kids had to get away from him as well. My husband was a lousy influence on them and I had to put a stop to this before the mental and spiritual damage to them was irreversible. My man wasn't worth sacrificing my children over.

I called Kenneth's three brothers and my sisters and brothers over to the house for support. I didn't want to be alone in the house when I told Kenneth that I was leaving his sorry ass and that he could kiss my ass. My kids were out of the house for their own safety. I left them with my father to protect them. Kenneth's three brothers Landon, Dylan and Lucas and my two sisters Abigail and Gabrielle and three brothers Nicolas, Nathan and Benjamin were at the house for support and protection. The eight of them promised to not let Kenneth physically attack me. There was nothing they could do about his big mouth though. His mouth was like a garbage truck. It was filled with garbage and he spit it out at me whenever he had a chance. Our brothers and sisters were all there as my bodyguards. All of them were at the agreement that the kids and I had to get away from this man.

"Are you alright?" my sister Gabrielle asked with great concern. "Why haven't you told any of us how bad things have gotten between you and Kenneth? We could have intervened a long time ago."

"Has he hit you?" my sister Abigail asked. "Has he ever hit my nephews and niece?"

"No. He has never hit me or any of the children. His words are so hurtful and venomous though that I just can't take it anymore. His constant mental and verbal abuse is rubbing off more and more on the kids also. The boys are starting to verbally abuse their little sister more than ever. They are learning this behavior from their father. How are they going to grow up and learn what the right way to treat and respect a woman is if the only role model they have is a man who treats his wife this way? I can actually picture them mentally or even physically abusing the women in their lives when they grow up. If things don't change for them they could actually wind up getting arrested when they become men for domestic abuse on their wives or girlfriends. You see it all the time in the news. Not only celebrities, but average men are accused each and every day of beating or even killing their wives and girlfriends. I won't have that happen to my sons. I will do whatever it takes to show them that this is not appropriate behavior. They are definitely going to need therapy after this. I think we all do."

"Even if he has never hit any of you, his verbal and emotional abuse has to stop now," my brother Benjamin said angrily. "He has no right to speak to a woman that way. Who the hell does he think he is? Nobody abuses my sister like this. He doesn't have a choice in the matter. Either he gets help or I will personally kick his ass. The choice is his."

Even Kenneth's brother's felt sorry for me and agreed to protect me. They loved him but felt like he needed help for his anger and insecurities before his abuse turned physical or even deadly. They were not only scared for me and the kids, but for him as well. They all remembered their father's alcoholism and verbal abuse that he subjected the family to when they were children. Their father got help years ago from anger management programs and from doctors for his alcoholism. He had redeemed himself and his wife and children had forgiven him. They were survivors and adjusted well. That is, all of them adjusted well except for my husband. He obviously didn't adjust at all to having an ex-alcoholic abusive father in his life. He had become his father. He had become an abuser himself. His father knew it and felt overwhelming guilt for it. By this time, all the family had seen and heard the abuse and was all disgusted by it. My husband's attacks brought back haunting memories to his parents of the time when their own family was dysfunctional with alcoholism and abuse.

"You have to understand what has happened to him Benjamin," Kenneth's brother Lucas responded. "We all grew up with our own father mentally and physically abusing us. It affected us all in different ways but I think it affected Kenneth the worst. I'm not making excuses for him, by no means. I understand that any abuse to a woman can't be tolerated and should never happen. I understand how angry you are that our brother has abused your sister. I'm just saying that our brother obviously needs psychiatric help. Getting his ass beat is not the solution. It will not solve anything. It could just make things worse for your sister and the kids."

"We're here to make sure that he gets the help that he needs," his brother Landon said. "Even if this marriage has to end in order for my brother to get help, than so be it. We will do whatever it takes to help him."

"Do you think that he is going to allow us to help him?" Dylan asked.

"He has no choice but to get help," said Landon. "He can't just be allowed to go through life abusing women. It's obvious that he needs help."

"My nephews and my niece can't go through life watching their mother being abused and watching their father act like an idiot either," Nicolas said angrily. "Our sister and those innocent children have suffered enough."

"I feel like whipping his ass for what he has put my sister through." Nathan said angrily.

"That's not why we were summoned here today," replied Lucas. "We came here to support your sister and to ensure that this situation doesn't become physically violent. None of us want that to happen."

"The only violence there is going to be is me whipping his ass for the way he has treated my sister!" Nathan yelled.

"Nathan please calm down," I pleaded. "I didn't call you all over here to beat up on my husband. I just need for me and the kids to get away from him so he can get the help he needs. He is not a bad man. He just has forgotten how to respect not only women, but himself as well. He is an unhappy and tormented man and I understand that had something to do with the abuse he endured as a child. I don't hate him. I feel sorry for him. He needs help. He needs the kind of help that I can't give him. Maybe now he will get that help. If he won't do it for himself, maybe he'll do it for our children."

"Well, even if he doesn't you and the kids are not going to stay with him," Gabrielle said with great concern. "Enough is enough. The abuse has to stop now."

"I think I hear him coming. His car just pulled up. Get ready folks. Let the intervention begin," Benjamin said.

As soon as my husband walked into the house the mental and verbal abuse began. It was almost as though he was thinking of ways to abuse me as he was walking up to the house.

"Teresa is dinner ready?"

"No. Not yet Kenneth," I replied. "We have to talk. I have some things I need to say to you. Please come in the living room."

"I had a long day Teresa. What the fuck do you want to talk about? You've been here all day long and dinner is not ready yet? I bet you just sat around on your fat ass all day long and nothing got done. Am I right Teresa? Were you sitting around on your fat ass stuffing your mouth with food so you could get fatter and fatter? You're such a worthless piece of shit!"

His abusive behavior had become somewhat ritualized. He was beginning to sound like a broke record. It was the same shit over and over again. He had begun to actually enjoy it. I was sick of him. He was starting to sound more and more stupid to me. I was over him and his abuse. His verbal shit didn't even hurt me anymore. I had become numb to it. He came into the living room and saw the family sitting around. He was totally surprised.

"Hey guys," he said with a confused look on his face. "We weren't expecting all of you over here tonight. What are all of you doing over here? What's going on?"

"We came here because your wife has some things to say to you and she needs us for moral support," his brother Landon said. "You need to shut up and listen for once."

"What the hell is going on here? I had a long day and I'm tired. What bullshit has she been filling your heads up with now? I only speak to my wife that way because I'm trying to make her into a better wife and mother. The more I yell at her, the better she gets. If I just left her alone she would sit around the house all day long and eat until she blows up to three hundred pounds. She's jeopardizing her health by eating so much. She could die if she keeps on eating the way she does. You want that to happen? Can't all of you see that by me verbally insulting her I am making her into a better woman? I am motivating her."

Dylan said, "Kenneth we have all heard on more than one occasion how you speak to your wife. There is nothing motivating about it. Not only has she had enough, but we've all had enough. You need help my brother. You need help now."

"What makes you think that calling a woman a stupid bitch or a fat cow is going to motivate her into being a better wife and mother?" my sister Abigail asked. "You can't be that ignorant. All you are accomplishing is destroying her self-esteem and the very essence of who she is as a woman. Don't you see that?"

"You need help brother-in-law," Gabrielle said. "You need help now before it is too late. What about the mental abuse that your children are experiencing everyday by watching their mother being abused like this? Do you not see that your behavior is influencing them and shaping the type of men your sons will turn out to be? Don't you realize that my beautiful niece will grow up believing that it is alright for a man to mentally or even physically abuse her? You need help now. Let us help you. We are not here to hurt you."

"I don't need any damn help. I just need my stupid ass wife to show me some respect. I'm the man of this house. Look how she respects me. She calls all of you over here and tells lies about me? What are you supposed to do? Are all of you going to kick my ass? Teresa if you weren't such a fat lazy-ass bitch we wouldn't be in this mess. You're such a stupid bitch!"

My sister Gabrielle stood up and yelled, "Kenneth you're not going to talk to my sister like that anymore. We have had about enough of listening to you abuse our sister. She is not going to tolerate your shit anymore. It's over. You're over."

"Gabrielle, it's time for me to stand up for myself," I said with renewed confidence. "You know what Kenneth? I've had enough of you talking to me like this. I'm not going to tolerate this shit anymore. If you can't respect me as a woman and as your wife then you need to get out. I don't want you anymore. I don't want to be married to you anymore. You need to go get you some skinny little bitch and leave me alone since I'm so fat. Our marriage is over. I don't want your sorry ass anymore and I don't want your ignorant influence around our kids. They deserve better than this. They deserve a better you and until you get help I am going to petition the courts to keep you away from them. They deserve to be around a man who knows how to treat a woman. I'm going to make sure they see exactly how a woman is to be treated. I refuse to allow you to abuse me right in front of them for one more second. Not only are you abusing me but you are abusing them as well. You are hurting them emotionally and as their mother I won't sit by and tolerate it any longer. It ends right now."

"What are you bitching about now Teresa?" Kenneth yelled. "You know you can't leave me. Look at you. You're a fat tub of lard that no other man will ever want. Look at yourself. You're fat and ugly. You're lucky I stayed with you. If I decide to leave your ugly ass you're gonna spend the rest of your life alone. No other man is ever going to marry your fat ass. The only other man you could ever get is a crack addict or a bum. No decent man is going to want you. You're nothing. You're nobody and you never will be."

I yelled right back at him, "You know what Kenneth, I'm sure there is another man out there who would be proud to be with a woman like me. Just because you don't know how to appreciate me doesn't mean that other men won't. I'm worth something. I am worth another man loving me and believe me I'm going to find him. My new man is going to treat me like a queen and show me how a woman is supposed to be loved. Do you really think that I am going to take the opinion of a low-life piece of shit like you? I tell you what, I'll take my chances. Even if I don't ever find another man it doesn't matter. I would rather spend the rest of my life alone than to spend one more second with your sorry ass. I have myself who I love and I have our three beautiful children. They are the true loves of my life. I also have God. Yes, I forgot him for a long time because I have been spending years putting up with your abuse instead of focusing my energy and time on my children and my relationship with God. That's going to change. All I need is my children and my God in heaven. I don't need more. I don't need you. Now, get out of here. I mean it Kenneth. Get out!"

"Teresa, do I really have to put my foot all the way up your ass because you know I'll do it?"

"You are not going to put your foot anywhere but on the floor," my brother Benjamin said sternly. "My brother and I are here to make damn sure that you don't lay a hand on our sister. You might as well put that shit right out of your head."

"You know what?" Kenneth asked. "Fuck this shit! I don't want you anyway Teresa. I don't need this. I can do much better than your fat ass. Have a good life being alone. No man is ever going to want you. I'm out of here."

"Ken you can come stay with me and Margaret," Kenneth's brother Landon said. "You can stay with us as long as you want as long as you promise to get help."

"I'm not staying with any of you bastards! You come over to my home and take that bitch's side over your own brother? Fuck all three of you!"

"Kenneth, don't be like this," Dylan said. "We only came over to help. We want to help both of you. We still love you man. That hasn't changed."

"What if we weren't here Kenneth?" Lucas said. "This situation could have gotten out of hand and you could be in jail right now. If you get physical with your wife you will be arrested. We're your brothers and we're not going to stand by and let that happen. Think about your kids, man."

Kenneth was furious. "Fuck this!" he said angrily. He went upstairs and packed a small suitcase. He came back downstairs and stormed out the door. He refused to say anything else to any of us. He was acting like a wounded dog. He went and stayed at one of his friend's houses. He refused any of his family's assistance or support. A few days later Kenneth called me and begged me to take him back. Part of me wanted to take him back but, I thought back to all the nasty things he said to me over the years and how he verbally abused me in private and in front of other people. I thought of how he abused me in front of our children and how he even tried to get them to agree with him. I thought about how my own sons were starting to verbally assault their own little sister and how she was cursing more and more like an angry man. I decided that there was no way I would ever go back to that.

Our marriage was over. I was finally done. I had become a woman toughened by betrayal and humiliation. I became strong. I became committed to ensuring the safety and well-being of my children. They became my inspiration and my only focus. I was ready to finally put my children first. Being without his constant verbal attacks was a breath of fresh air. It was truly liberating. I didn't feel like I was carrying around a ten ton boulder on my shoulders. I no longer had someone abating and verbally abusing me constantly. I came to the realization that my happiness had to come from within me. It couldn't come from someone else. I had to love myself before I could have a healthy relationship with someone else. I gave me and my children time to breathe and enjoy life again. I gave us all time to heal. I had become so dependent financially on my husband that I had to re-learn sustainability and survival techniques in order to support my children. I went back to school and studied to become a social worker. Now, I am able to counsel other women who are themselves struggling to get out of their abusive relationships. I said good-bye to the old, scared, low self-esteemed me and embraced the confident, successful woman that I had become. I was whole again. I was phenomenal.

For a long time I was extremely resentful of the way my children had been mentally abused and how my husband's negative influence had affected them. The resentment that I felt would have eventually destroyed me. I had to let it go. He wasn't worth the energy that resentment took. For my children's sake I forgave him. I had to regain my perspective on life, love and what it took for my happiness. I realized something. It took the peace and happiness of my children to help me realize just what life was all about. Watching them become happier made me happy. Their joy was my joy. My fear of enjoying life began to dissipate. I embraced life. Eventually my husband did get psychological help for his anger and help for his alcoholism. The humiliation he felt on that particular day almost destroyed him but he survived. He was beginning to heal from the self-destructive urges that had destroyed his childhood and turned him into the abusive man that he was today.

We did divorce and I got full custody of the children. He got visitation rights on weekends. We never said anything negative about each other to the kids again. My husband apologized to the kids and told them that he would always love their mommy. I allowed them to have a relationship with their daddy but as for me, I wasn't interested in ever taking him back. I loved myself too much. I wanted and felt that I deserved emotional fulfillment and I could never get that from him. My children were finally happy after receiving extensive counseling. The ubiquitous melancholy that we all felt throughout the house for years was gone. There was joy and laughter now. It took me years to develop a zero tolerance for any man mentally abusing my children and now that I was finally at that point it simply would never be allowed again. I decided to exercise my God-given right not to be abused in any way by another man. It didn't matter any longer to me if I had to spend the rest of my life alone. My children would be protected. My unconditional love for my children was my inspiration to go on with life. I did it for them. I embraced my freedom from my abusive man. I felt miraculously rejuvenated. I felt as though God had his hands on my life. I immersed myself with raising my children. I embrace life the way God wanted me to. I embraced the call to return to my Christian roots and serve our God.

Chapter 2

LADIES, HAVE ANY of you had a man leave you for another woman? Has your man ever cheated on you? What if you came home late from a hard day at work and found your boyfriend, husband or fiancé in your bed having sex with another woman? What would you do? What if the woman he was having sex with was your best friend? Would you invite the woman over for tea? I'm writing this letter to all my sisters around the world who have been cheated on by a man and/or emotionally abused. I understand exactly what you're going through. Ladies, it's not your fault. A woman can be emotionally abused by the man she's in a relationship with. You've heard the old saying, 'Ignorance is bliss!' Well, it isn't when it comes to love. It isn't bliss when it comes to love and romance and your man betrays you and hurts you to the point where it destroys the very essence of who you are. He broke my heart and my spirit. I was inconsolable. The Ricky and Vanessa that everyone thought existed was gone. In fact, the more I think about it the more I realize that it was all an illusion. It only existed in my mind. There really never was a Ricky and Vanessa. There was a Ricky, Vanessa, Tanya, Brenda, and whoever else he was screwing behind my back. My man was very cunning in trying to hide his affairs and for awhile he got away with them.

I had been completely deceived. In retrospect, the signs of his cheating were all there. Ladies, the signs of their cheating is always there. We just need to open our eyes and look. Some of you know exactly what I'm talking about. My man was acting like an international playboy when in fact; he wasn't all that. He was just an asshole from Atlanta, Georgia who had absolutely no respect for women. His behavior was calculating and conniving. You have to understand. His cheating at the very beginning was inconspicuous. He left no clues or hints that he was cheating on me. He was good at lying to me. Later there were definite signs that I chose to ignore or were blinded to. He was inconsistent with his love. I didn't know which way was up and which way was down. I had a lot of self-doubt at that time. I was a fool. I did not want to be presumptuous in believing that he was cheating on me when I didn't have any proof. In retrospect there was plenty of proof. I just chose to ignore it. In my mind I only had suspicions and speculations. He had become such a manipulative bastard.

Everyone told me that I was a beautiful woman. Hell, even I had thought that I was pretty. But, at the moment I found out that Ricky was cheating on me I felt like nothing. I felt that I was not good enough for any man. I felt ugly and stupid. What was wrong with me? How could I allow myself to be emotionally abused like this? I realize now that it is never a good idea to let a man take complete control over the essence of who you are. Don't let him take away your spirit and soul and convert you into the woman he wants you to be. Be true to yourself and let the world see who you truly are. It's ok to lift each other up in the relationship but it's not ok to allow a man to beat you down spiritually and mentally. Ladies you know exactly what I'm talking about. Please do not be my judge and jury. I am not the only one. There are millions of women all over the world just like me. In retrospect I really knew that he was cheating on me deep down in my soul. I had to face the reality that a lot of women all over the world have to face each and every day, that my man is a cheater. Have you ever had a gut feeling screaming for you to leave him but you stayed anyway? That sweet, kind, nurturing spirit that God gave us women whispered in your ear for you to stay with him and try to work things out. You ignored your gut feeling that told you to leave and you stayed with him. Many of you have heard that whisper telling you to leave but you stayed with your man. Women all over the world know exactly what I'm talking about. Many of you are hearing that soft whisper right now. It's telling you to not give up and just stay with your man. It's telling you that somehow you are going to change him. You feel it in your heart and spirit. Many of you knew that your man was cheating on you but you ignored it. You convinced yourselves that it was all in your imaginations and that your man was faithful to you. You convinced yourselves that he loved you and only you and would never cheat on you. I understand. I was you.

I loved Ricky and I would do anything to please him. I was actually enabling my man to be a cheater. I turned my back to his activities and pretended that they weren't happening. I gave and gave into the relationship but Ricky gave nothing. What a selfish son-of-a-bitch! He had become deceitful, narcissistic and callous. He started treating me as one of his possessions, one of his things. I must have been the stupidest woman on earth. I told myself that no other woman could have been that dumb. But, now I realize that what women are going through with their no-good-men has nothing whatsoever to do with stupidity. God made us to love and trust. It is the essence of what a woman is. God gave men that same quality and I know a lot of you are wondering what happened to them. The truth of the matter is that the number of women on this earth outnumbers men and there are women out in the world who don't care if your man is married or in a relationship. They need a man in their lives and your man will do just fine. They would rather have your man than no man at all. And the men just can't seem to resist them. It's easy, free and quick sex that they can have at any moment without you ever finding out. Or so they seem to think. The truth always comes out. That is the moment that people get hurt and their worlds get turned upside down. Relationships get destroyed and there is no turning back.

I just knew in my heart that no man would ever want to be with just me. I felt that I wasn't good enough for another man. I lost faith in myself and in men. They could never be trusted. I would never put my trust or my life in the hands of a man ever again. No man had ever hurt me the way that Ricky did. He stomped over my love and my heart and made a complete fool out of me. Why did I trust him? Why did I love him? How could I ever love another man again? I tried everything I could to please Ricky but he never seemed to be satisfied. I was not enough for him. He wanted more. But, he wanted more of what? I don't think even Ricky knew exactly what he wanted. I realize now that I wasn't the problem. Ricky was the problem. He was a cheater and he emotionally abused me. He not only crushed my spirit but he took away the very essence of me. His cheating began to take a tremendous toll on my emotions. I began to forget who I was. I lost confidence in myself as one of God's children. I lost myself. I dived into a state of self-pity. He destroyed our relationship. He almost destroyed me. I became depressed and even contemplated suicide. He had become toxic to me. He gave me gifts to hide his cheating. The gifts that he gave me were nothing but things. They were not a suitable substitute for the love, respect and compassion that I craved from him. They weren't enough to appease the loneliness that I felt.

His cheating destroyed us. It wasn't my fault. I had to get rid of him once and for all.

I had to do a complete overview of our relationship. I was sick of his cheating, his lying and his narcotic addiction. I was sick of him. I had to face the unavoidable truth that my man was cheating on me. I dug deep down within my soul and found the strength that God had given me. I told myself that I was strong and independent. I told myself that I was a phenomenal woman. Ladies, listen to me. That strength is inside all of us. Think back to the time in your life when you were full of faith in Jesus and you felt truly blessed by him. You read your bible religiously. You attended church regularly. You prayed at night before you went to bed and lifted your hands up in the morning to glorify the Lord. Then you met your man and because of years of abuse you forgot that you were the daughters of a mighty God. Maybe you felt abandoned by God. Maybe the very essence of who you were has been crushed so low that you didn't have the emotional or spiritual strength to pick up your bible and pray. God never abandoned you. He saw it all. He saw every slap, punch and kick you endured. God saw every time he cheated on you with another woman. God saw it. One day your man will have to stand before a mighty God and he has a lot of explaining to do. God heard every time your man verbally and physically abused you. He saw your tears, felt your pain and heard your cries. He felt your sadness and loneliness. Sometimes the strength within us is hidden by years of having self-doubt and self-hatred. Don't be mistaken. It is still there. I used the strength and the rage that I felt for him betraying and humiliating me to throw his sorry ass out of my life. But I still have feelings for him. Oh God please help me. After everything this two-timing son-of-a-bitch has done I still love him. Ladies, please do not judge me. There are millions of women all over the world just like me who have been cheated on by their men. I am not alone. We are as one.

—————

Ricky sat on the side of the bed with his feet on the floor. He was already high as shit from drinking rum and coke and snorting cocaine. He reached over to the side table and grabbed his pants. He pulled out a small container of white powder from his pants pocket and then threw his pants back on the table. He called the white powder his white beauty. He loved that shit more than life itself. Nothing meant more to him, not even the women in his life. But Ricky would never allow one of his women to snort cocaine. If he ever caught one of his women snorting he would whip her ass. He was willing to sacrifice everything including his career, finances, and relationships just to have a taste of that shit. He gently and slowly poured a small amount of the cocaine onto a line on top of the side table next to the bed. He leaned over, placed one finger over his nostril and snorted the cocaine up into his right nostril. He took one finger and wiped it over the area on the table where the cocaine had been. He put the finger in his mouth so he could get every single drop of it. He didn't want any of it to go to waste. He closed his eyes as the cocaine traveled throughout his body taking him to a state of total ecstasy. To Ricky, this was better than having sex. Then he opened his eyes, turned to the woman lying next to him and they made love.

Ricky had gone out that Saturday night to a club in Atlanta without me. He told me some bullshit story about how he was going to spend the evening with business associates. He obviously was being deceitful. His arrogance was indisputable. He believed that he could just do anything that he wanted to no matter how much it could hurt me. He didn't give a damn. He saw the woman at the bar and sat down next to her. She looked over at him and smiled. He reciprocated.

"Can I buy you a drink?" he asked.

"Sure honey," she said. "Why not? Thank you."

He waved his finger at the bartender Art Wright.

"What can I get for you man?" Art asked.

"Yeah man. Get me a gin and tonic and get the lady another of what she's drinking."

The bartender smiled and said, "Ok man. It's coming right up." Art brought their drinks to them and Ricky paid him.

"Would you like to dance?" Ricky asked as they took sips from their drinks.

"Sure honey. I'd love to dance with you."

He led her onto the dance floor and held her tightly. She smiled as he gazed into her eyes. Meanwhile, back in our apartment I took a shower, turned the light off and went to bed alone again. As I lay in bed I thought of my man at his boring business dinner trying to convince clients to hire his law firm. I was convinced he wanted to be with me but he couldn't. In actuality he was trying to get into the panties of the no-named woman. They danced slowly with their bodies pressed up against one another. There was no space between them. Their pelvises pressed into one another. She closed her eyes and enjoyed his manhood. I fell asleep with my man on my mind.

She had smoky eyes and bright red pouty lips. He whispered in her ear, "You're a very sexy woman and you are very beautiful. You want to go back to your place? I'd love to spend the evening with you."

"Yes. Yes I would. I'd love to spend the evening with you. Come on sugar," she said in a sweet sexy voice. She held Ricky's hand and led him out of the club.

"Do you have a car?" Ricky asked.

"No. A friend gave me a ride here."

"Come on. Let's take my car. I'll drive," Ricky responded. He drove her in his car to her apartment. Once they entered the apartment they started kissing each other passionately. Ricky started to pull her clothes off of her. She in turn started to undress him. He kissed and caressed her breasts tenderly. They never made it to the bedroom. They made love right on the floor. After they finished they went to bed to rest and sober up. He didn't even remember her name and he didn't care. She was just a piece of ass to him. She was just some bitch that he had picked up at the club who was easy enough to spread her legs and give him what he needed that night. She had served her purpose and now he was done with her. The no-named woman thought that because he was making love to her that he would be hers forever. After they finished resting, Ricky got out of her bed and got dressed.

"Where are you going so fast honey?" she asked as she sat up in bed. "I thought we were gonna spend some time together? Hey, maybe we could go out and get something to eat. Or, if you want I could whip you up a meal and we could eat in. What do you think?"

"I have to go home to my woman," he replied non-caringly. "She's waiting for me. I don't want her to get suspicious. She turns into a total bitch if I show up too late. I'm not in the mood for her shit tonight."

"You didn't tell me you had a woman," she said with disappointment. "I thought you were alone. I thought I was your woman tonight."

"You were my woman for about five minutes," he responded coldly. "Now it's over and you're over. I have to go." He put his coat on, reached in his wallet and pulled out fifty dollars and threw it on the bed.

She pulled the sheet up over her breasts and cried out, "You bastard! You miserable self-righteous asshole!" she yelled.

"And then some," he said with a smirk on his face. He walked out of the apartment and left her sitting up in bed alone. As he was walking out he mumbled underneath his breath, "What a fucking waste of time. The stupid bitch made a lousy piece of ass anyway." He couldn't believe he had wasted any expenditure of time on this useless woman. Ricky had an inculpable attitude. He felt like he didn't owe any woman anything. He didn't want to be emotionally committed to any woman. The no-named woman picked up the fifty dollars and threw it across the room. She felt like she was no more than a piece of meat and she felt ashamed. As for Ricky, he really didn't give a damn.

I was twenty-four years old and a single woman. I met Ricky one night when a couple of my co-workers from the advertising agency where we worked and I decided to go out on the town. It was ladies night in all the clubs which meant that we could get into our favorite club for free. We were looking to be bad and have a good time on that particular night. My friends and I were the epitome of glamour and elegance. We were like flowers in full bloom. We knew a lot about fashion and it was reflective in the way we dressed. My three best friends were my soul mates and the very mirror image of me. We were as one. We had the same souls, the same spirits, the same tastes, the same likes and dislikes. We were sisters in spirit if not biologically. You'll see later that I overestimated my so-called friends. My name is Vanessa and many consider me to be very beautiful, very sexy, and having an outgoing personality. When I walked into a room all eyes were on me. I knew how to dress and how to carry myself like a lady. My hair and makeup was always impeccable. My friends and I walked into the club and stood in the doorway to check out the scene and to be checked out by everyone in the club, especially the men. My friends and I were looking good. Our hair and makeup was perfect. We were looking fierce with our stiletto high heels and sexy short dresses. My friends and I posed at the front of the club for a few minutes so that everyone could see us. We had the silhouette of goddesses. The glow of youth and beauty emanated from our faces. We were divas and we knew it. The men turned and looked at us because they wanted to be with us. The women looked at us because they wanted to be us. We walked into the club and went to an empty table.

A fine waiter came over to our table and said, "Hello beautiful ladies. Can I get you something to drink?"

"I'll have a glass of white wine," I said.

"I'll have some rum and coke," Barbara said.

My friend Wanda started to flirt shamelessly with the waiter. "Hey bring me a shot of gin and juice," she said in a sexy voice. She smiled and asked, "Hey what's your name sweetie?"

"My name is Walter," he replied. It was obvious that he was interested in her and was enjoying her flirtatious behavior.

Wanda turned to us and winked her eye. She was amused by him. At that moment he was her toy. She turned to the waiter and asked, "Walter huh. Well Walter, my name is Wanda and I think you're hot."

"I think you're hot too," Walter whispered. He looked as though at any moment he was going to start drooling over her. He was trying too hard to impress and in actuality was making a fool of himself.

Wanda leaned close to him and put her arm around his shoulder. She took her other hand and started to stroke his cheek. She put her lips close to his mouth and pretended as though she was going to kiss him with her sweet succulent red lips. He could smell her sweet perfume and for a second he closed his eyes and enjoyed her sweet aroma and the softness of her delicate hand. His heart started to beat faster and we all could tell that he was getting turned on. We smiled at each other but did not say a word.

"Honey why don't you go to the bar and bring me an Apple Martini," Wanda whispered in a soft sexy voice. "I need something to quench my thirst." She started to lick her lips and made jesters as though she was sucking on a penis which turned the waiter on even more.

I'll be right back with your drinks ladies," the waiter whispered. He almost tripped as he hurried to the bar to get our drinks. All four of us laughed out loud.

"Wanda you're a hot mess," Charlotte said sarcastically. "Damn you're such a whore."

Wanda laughed and said, "Charlotte shut up. I know you're not calling me a hot mess with all the men you've teased and made a fool out of. You've screwed more men than all the football teams and basketball teams put together. You're the whore."

"Shut up Wanda," Charlotte said angrily. We all laughed out loud.

"I think he's sweet," Barbara said.

"He acts like he's a virgin," Charlotte said sarcastically. "You'd think that he's never been with a woman before. I wonder if he's gay."

"A man like that can't be gay," Wanda responded. "Have mercy! That's one fine man."

"These days you really can't tell who is gay and who is straight," I said to the ladies. "Besides, there is nothing wrong with being gay. Don't be ignorant."

"I never said there was anything wrong with being gay," Wanda responded angrily. "I mean no disrespect. I have a lot of gay friends and you know that. Don't even try to put me in the category with gay haters because all of you know better."

There were a lot of fine men in the club that night. I hadn't dated for a while since I ended my relationship with Mitch several months ago. I was getting lonely. Mitch was a sweet guy, but he was boring as hell. Dating him was like watching wet paint dry. Mitch was cute but he wasn't all that. He had been in and out of relationships before he met me and now I know why. He had no idea how to treat a woman and make her happy. He was too into himself and his broke-ass friends. His friends didn't have jobs. They didn't have cars and most of them still lived with their mamas. Ladies, you've met men like this and you know exactly what I'm talking about. Ladies, have any of you been in a relationship with a man who had best friends that were over your house so much it was as though they had moved in? Mitch's best friends Willy, Bubba, Antwoine and Quandell spent every Saturday afternoon hanging around my house with him. They watched sports and drank beer all afternoon. Of course I paid for their beer, made them snacks and brought the food and drink to them like their servant. I even cleaned up their mess when they were done. Ladies, what the hell was I thinking? Damn I was a fool! Mitch never wanted to do anything with me. He was happy just sitting around the house with one hand holding a cold beer and the other stuffed down his pants so he could scratch himself like a dog. He never wanted to go out and would get mad and jealous when I wanted to go out. One Saturday evening I was bored as hell. We weren't doing anything interesting so I asked Mitch, "Honey, why don't we go out to the club? I feel like dancing. I want to have some fun. Let's not even think about it. Let's just get dressed and get the hell out of here."

"Is that all you think about?" Mitch asked angrily. "All you want to do is dress up like a whore and shake your ass in front of a bunch of other fucking dudes. Why do you always want to act like such a whore?"

I was shocked. "What did you just say to me?" I asked with a surprised look on my face. "Who do you think you're talking to like that? I am a woman and you will show me some respect."

"You heard me woman," he responded like an idiot. "We're not going anywhere. We're staying in tonight. If you want to shake your ass you can do it for me. Why don't you shake your ass on into the kitchen and bring me a beer?"

I just stood there and stared at him for a minute. I thought to myself, "What am I doing here with this jerk? He's a dog that doesn't even deserve me. What a low-life idiot." I then told him to get off of his ass, go in the kitchen, get his self an ice-cold beer and shove it all the way up his ass! I had finally had enough and told him that it was over. I ended the relationship with Mitch. This fool had the nerve to tell me that I was making a huge mistake, that he was the best thing that ever happened to me and that no other man would ever want me. Is he deluding himself or what? He then had the nerve to tell me that he was actually dumping me because he was better than me. Is he kidding? Can any man possibly be this stupid? This is the same guy who can't hold down a job, can't stay in a relationship with a woman and who after I dumped him had no place to go but back to his mama. I knew I could do better. I wanted someone who knew how to treat me like a woman. Mitch was crushed, but I had to do what was right for me. But, now I was ready to start a new relationship. I was tired of being alone. It was not only time for me to get a man but it was time for me to get laid.

My big mouthed friend Wanda said, "Damn! Look at all these fine men in here tonight. Even you could get laid on a night like tonight Barbara."

"Kiss my ass Wanda," she said as she stuck her middle finger up in Wanda's face.

We all laughed. Let me tell you, my friends were something else. Wanda always spoke what was on her mind. At times she didn't give a damn whose feelings she hurt. She didn't think before she opened her mouth. There were times when her big mouth got her into trouble and a few times she almost got her ass kicked. But she was also very funny and always the life of the party. She worked at the advertising firm as a business attorney and was well respected in the company. My friend Barbara was a very intelligent and ambitious young woman. She was very pretty and the youngest advertising executive in the company. She was one of the Executive Vice Presidents in Charge of Marketing and Sales. She had earned her Bachelor's degree with a major in business administration and a minor in marketing. She was very successful in her professional life. But, as for her personal life, that was very different. Barbara sacrificed her personal and love life to get to where she was today. She worked long hours, sometimes twelve to thirteen hours a day and was able to break through the so-called 'glass ceiling' and climb the corporate ladder quickly. She did it with her mind not by laying on her back.

We teased her from time to time saying things like, "Damn Barbara, you must have spider webs on your pussy by now." Or we would say, "If you don't get laid soon your pussy is gonna shrivel up and dry up like a prune."

Barbara would always point out that it was she who owned a half a million dollar home and drove a brand new seventy-five thousand dollar sports car. I had to admit it. The bitch had it going on.

My friend Charlotte was the only one of the group that dated a lot. When I say a lot, I mean a lot! I don't want to come right out and say that she was a whore, but she must have had sex with at least half the men in the city of Atlanta, Georgia. She wasn't ashamed of it either. "Why is it that when a man dates a lot of women he is a stud?" she would ask. "He's the man. But when a woman dates a lot she's a whore. Why is it ok for men to see a lot of women but not ok for a woman to do the same? Who made that rule? Men!"

Charlotte didn't feel she needed to apologize to anyone for being who she was. Her philosophy was that people need to worry about the fucked up relationships they're in and stop worrying about who she's sleeping with. She dated a lot of fine successful men too. She was always honest and upfront with them in that she was not ready or willing to get into an exclusive one-on-one relationship with any man at that time. Ladies, you know that a man is a dog and as long as he can get some sex he doesn't care, so they were able and willing to give her what she wanted. In fact, most of them were relieved that she didn't want a one-on-one exclusive relationship. It gave them the freedom to sleep with her and then run back to their women without getting caught. Charlotte worked at our firm as a marketing agent. Her job was to bring in clients to our firm. Most times she used her college educated brain to bring in clients. At times she brought in clients by resting on her back with her legs open. It wasn't a job requirement but that was Charlotte going above and beyond the call of duty. Charlotte thought that because she dated a lot she knew everything there was to know about men. She would say that there are several types of men in the world. First, there are the players who want to go around and sleep with everything in site. If it has a vagina then they'll sleep with it. Then there are the users. These men are the ones that will ask a woman out on a date and then ask her if she has any money to pay for it because he's a little short on cash. These men are also the same ones that wait around every week for their girlfriend's paychecks or every month for their girl's welfare checks instead of getting up off of their lazy asses and getting a job themselves. These men are the same ones that have little tots running around from different women and don't pay child support for any of them. They are not only destroying their own lives but that of their children as well. What kind of example are they being to their children? How can their sons grow up to respect women and become real men when their own dads are nothing but lazy losers?

Then there are the men who are gay and admit it. They will tell you in a second that they just aren't sexually turned on by women. They are in love with other men and are not ashamed to let the world know it. They refuse to be disrespected or treated any differently than anyone else. They are their own men. I have a lot more respect for a man who isn't trying to live a double life. The men living double-lives are the down-low-men. These are the men that I don't have respect for. There is an undercover world of men who keep their sexual relationships with other men secret from their wives and girlfriends. They are living a double life. Their women are usually either totally clueless to what he is doing or are in total denial. These men don't want to be thought of as gay. They tell themselves that they are not gay because they don't live the gay lifestyle. These guys could be anyone. They could be a lawyer, a businessman, or a garbage man. He could be anyone anywhere. Because of the pressures in society they are not able or refuse to admit that they are gay. Instead, they live a fake ass heterosexual life trying to fool everyone in their lives. These men are dishonest with their wives, girlfriends and maybe even themselves. These are the men that have sex with other men and then come home and have sex with their women potentially exposing them to AIDS and other STD's.

Then there are the men that Charlotte called, "Mama's Boys." These are the men who let mama control not only them, but their relationships as well. These men are in their twenties, hell maybe even in their thirties and still live at home with their mamas. Anything they need mama provides for it. Mama is still feeding them, clothing them and cleaning up after them. Charlotte said that she wouldn't be surprised if their mamas wiped their asses after they shit. If mama didn't like the women that they were dating, watch out! Mama turns into a total psychopathic bitch and tries everything she can to break the relationship up. Ladies, have any of you been in a relationship with a man and had his mama interfere with your relationship to the point where you had to break up with him? To make matters worse, the men usually listens to mama and takes her side instead of sticking by the women that they're suppose to love. But let's face it; momma is paying for everything so why would he turn on the hand that feeds him? They say dumb things like, "This is my mama and I have to respect her opinion." Have any of you ever had a man that took his mother's side over you? Charlotte's response to this is that she doesn't have a problem with a man respecting his mama. Her problem is the men that respect their mamas at the expense of the women that they're supposed to be in love with. What about showing a little respect for your woman? Ladies, have any of you ever been in a relationship with a mama's boy and his mother got on your last nerves? Did you want to strangle the bitch or what?

Finally, there is one last classification of men according to Charlotte. According to her these are the men that every woman should want. They are the 'good men.' These men come from all walks of life. It doesn't matter what job they have or how much money they make because no matter what, these men will stick by their women. They don't walk away from their children and leave their woman struggling to be a single mom. He's faithful, a great father and his number one priority in life is keeping his family together. Believe it or not ladies these men do exist. But ladies let me ask you one question. Where the fuck are they hiding? Because, I swear I can't find one!

At the club that night Charlotte did her usual thing. She said, "Ok Ladies. Let's play the game. Let's see what kind of losers we have in here tonight."

"Here she goes again," Barbara said sarcastically.

Charlotte looked around the room. She pointed to a few men and gave a critique of just how much of a loser she thought they were. The first man she saw was wearing a wedding band. An idiot could tell that he was married. When he thought that no one was looking he slipped the wedding band off his finger and dropped it in his jacket pocket.

"A cheater!" we all said at the same time. We all laughed out loud. Come on ladies. Be honest. How many of you have walked into a club and was hit on by a man that you knew was married or had a significant other? He was looking good and smelling sexy and knew just the right words to get you hoping that he was the one. All the other women in the club wanted him but he was interested only in you. He asked for your number and you gladly gave it to him. Then you asked for his number and the bull-shit began. He came up with all kinds of stupid reasons why he couldn't give his number to you. Let me give you some examples.

He said, "I can't give you my number baby. I just had my home fumigated." How about this excuse? "I can't give you my number because I have a roommate who doesn't allow guests." My favorite is this. "I can't give you my number because my mama just got into town and she is staying at my house." Ladies don't walk away from him. Run! At that moment you just knew he was married or in a relationship. Oh, and I know some of you have met men who spend every weekend out with his boys in the club buying drink after drink for some trick even though they have a child at home who needs milk and diapers. Their women have to practically beg, steal and borrow to support their child while their men are acting like whores in the clubs. The next guy Charlotte pointed to was checking out the men in the club more than we were. The next guy was looking in the mirror at himself checking out how good looking he was.

"If this man is so much in love with himself, how the hell could he possibly take time to love a woman?" Charlotte asked. "She would be too much competition for him."

The next guy was hitting on every woman in the club. He was using the same weak-assed pick up line for every woman that he hit on. He was so pathetic that he mistakenly used the same pick up line for the same woman more than once. What an idiot.

We looked at each other and said out loud, "A player."

"No, no!" Wanda said sarcastically. "A loser!"

"Yeah, you're right," I responded in agreement as I laughed. "This guy doesn't give a damn who he sleeps with tonight as long as he gets some. He has no respect for women or himself. He probably doesn't have anything going for himself."

The last guy she pointed to was trying to get the women in the club to buy him a drink. We all looked at each other and said at the same time, "Broke ass brother." We laughed out loud again. The waiter came back with our drinks.

"Here you go beautiful ladies," he said. He gave each of us the drink that we had ordered and we reached for our money.

Barbara asked Charlotte, "Bitch do you need for me to pay for your drink, with your broke ass self?"

"Kiss my ass Barbara." Charlotte responded back to her.

We all laughed out loud again. We each paid the waiter what we owed for our drink. Wanda and the waiter looked at each other. Wanda put her finger in her mouth and began to suck on it as though she was having oral sex. The waiter tripped and almost fell as he hurried away. We all laughed out loud.

I looked around the room as I sipped on my drink. A couple of guys looked over at us and smiled. They had on baggy pants, hats on their heads as though they were in a gang and had gold teeth in their mouths. They were grown men trying to look like street thugs. It was pathetic. Why would any of us want to be with someone like that? They thought they were cool but they actually looked like fools. My girls and I looked at each other and laughed.

I whispered, "My god. I don't think so. I know we can do better than that."

There were a lot of people on the dance floor and the music sounded good. I looked over in the corner of the club and there he was. Ricky. This man was gorgeous. He was tall, handsome and very well dressed in an Italian suit. Ricky noticed me at the same time that I noticed him. Our eyes met and we smiled at each other. I was enraptured by him. I felt like I was in the middle of a fairy tale dream and couldn't wake up. I didn't want to wake up. I felt hypnotized by not only his sexuality but by the desire that was building up within me. It was like love at first sight. He started to walk toward us.

My friend Charlotte whispered, "Fine dude alert. Ladies, look what's coming our way. How do I look? Is my makeup ok?" She pulled out her mirror and checked herself out to see if her hair and makeup was presentable.

As he walked by, all the other women in the club checked him out. They wanted him as badly as I did. But, he was coming to me. I knew he was going to be mine. He knew he was looking good. You could see his confidence by the way he walked and carried himself. He walked over to us and introduced himself to me and my friends.

He looked at me and said, "Hello. My name is Ricky. It's a pleasure to meet you."

We all said at the same time, "Hi."

"I've come to rescue you," Ricky said as he looked me up and down.

"Really. You've come to rescue me from what?"

"I've come to rescue you from possibly spending a boring evening with one of the losers in this club," he replied with confidence.

"As opposed to spending the evening with a loser such as yourself?" I asked sarcastically.

"Hey, I'm no loser," he said with amusement.

"Then just what are you?" I asked curiously.

"I'm a successful lawyer working for a major law firm downtown and soon I hope to make partner. I'm also a gentleman who knows exactly how to treat a woman and show her a good time. Give me a chance to prove it to you. Would you like to dance?"

He reached out a hand to me. Wanda who was sitting right next to me pushed my shoulder hard enough to force me onto my feet. I took Ricky's hand gently. As I did, I turned around and gave Wanda a mean facial expression. Charlotte closed her eyes, leaned forward and smelled the back of his jacket as he walked by. She wanted to smell his sexiness. He smelled so good.

Barbara pulled her back to the table and whispered sternly, "Charlotte! Behave yourself."

"What? The man smells good," Charlotte said innocently. "I just wanted to get a whiff. Have mercy!" she whispered. "He is so fine and smells so good. I'll take that for myself. If that bitch doesn't want him then I'll damn sure take him."

I joined Ricky on the dance floor. At first the DJ played a fast song and we smiled at each other as we danced. Then a slow song was played. Ricky held me tightly and pressed his body against mine. I pressed my face gently against his and closed my eyes. He smelled so good and I hadn't felt this way for months. For a moment I felt my knees weaken and I thought my legs were going to buckle from underneath me. I needed this moment and I embellished in it. Ricky could sense how I felt and being a man he was pleased. He smiled to himself. I found him to be truly romantic and full of passion. I would later find out that he was also an affectionate lover. After we finished dancing Ricky walked me back to the table and ordered a round of drinks for all of us. He spent the rest of the evening at our table and he showed us that he was a gentleman and knew exactly how to show a woman a good time. He appeared to be the perfect man. I thought that I was the luckiest woman on the earth and that no woman could find a man such as this. I began to daydream about the first time we would kiss and the first time we would make love. I needed him. I had to have him. He looked over at me and smiled. It appeared to me that he really gave a damn. I would soon find out that he didn't give a damn about me or any other woman.

Ricky and I dated for several months before we moved in together. I didn't realize it at the time but Ricky was not really committed to the relationship. He was totally full of shit! He told me over and over that he loved me. He was a liar. I didn't mean anything to him. I was just someone he could temporarily set up house with. At first everything was wonderful. There are a lot of men in the world who are using women the same damn way. They only want a place to lay their heads. They want someone to cook for them, clean for them, and take care of the household responsibilities while they run the streets screwing every trick in sight. I know that some of you women have met the same type of assholes I am referring to. Ricky and I found a beautiful colonial style two bedroom apartment not far from my job. We decided to turn the second room into an office for him. He told me that he needed space to work and the second room was perfect. He needed a second room alright. He needed a second room to snort cocaine in. The bastard! I didn't realize it at the time, but that damn office was the beginning of Ricky taking over the apartment and my life. Eventually he would reduce me to nothing. There would be no sign of my existence anywhere. The decor of our condo was somewhat modern Bohemian and avant garde which was the way Ricky wanted it. The furnishings in the apartment were all hand-carved by skilled artisans that he had found in the art deco district. My tastes in decor didn't matter to him. I wanted Ricky to be comfortable so I sold the majority of the furniture in my old apartment at a garage sale and we moved the majority of Ricky's things into the new apartment. Wouldn't you ladies do the same thing to please your man? I was willing to do anything to enhance our relationship. I was willing to do anything to please my man. If I had only known that he was my man and every other bitch in the city's man I wouldn't have bothered.

Unknowingly, I had begun to sacrifice my spirit and soul to please that bastard. I unknowingly was beginning to give up my identity. At first I wasn't cognizant of the fact that he was taking over my life. I did what I had to do as a woman to make my man happy. I had breakfast ready for him every morning. I kept the apartment extra clean. Ricky was completely anal. He was rigorously disciplined yet deceptively callous at the same time. He wanted everything in its place at all times. Nothing could be out of place. But yet, his life was totally fucked up! What a contradiction. He would get upset if even one glass wasn't washed out immediately, dried and put back in its exact place. But, the fact that he was destroying our relationship didn't matter. I picked up his clothes from the dry cleaners. I had a hot meal ready for him every night even if he didn't show up to eat it. What a stupid bitch I was! I even hosted dinner parties for him whenever he invited friends and colleagues over.

I didn't realize it at the time but Ricky was screwing the majority of women friends and colleagues that I had entertained in my home. Ricky actually had sex with some of these women in my bed when I was away. I was putting all of me into the relationship. He was slowly becoming a self-centered jerk who didn't give a damn about me or any of the other women he screwed. To Ricky, women were just things. They were property that he possessed that could be gotten rid of at any time like old clothes. He was such a narcissist that he wasn't even capable of loving a woman the way she needed to be loved. He was too much in love with himself.

One evening Ricky said as he walked to the front door, "I have to go out for a minute and get a pack of cigarettes. I'll probably stop off and see a friend of mine who lives near here. We went to graduate school together. It won't take me long. I'll be back later." Ricky often walked around the corner for cigarettes or snacks so I thought nothing of it. Ricky walked into the apartment complex and knocked on the door. The door opened and my best friend Wanda with the big mouth stood in the doorway. She was naked underneath her short, sexy baby doll nightie.

"Damn girl you look good," Ricky said as he looked her up and down.

She smiled and took him into her arms. He held her tightly and kissed her passionately. He put his hand on her ass and pulled her close to him. She reached over and closed the front door as they stumbled into the apartment. They were still kissing as they made their way toward the bedroom. They never made it there. He made love to her right on the stairs. She pulled his shirt off as he began to pull his pants and underwear down. They continued to kiss each other and then he penetrated her. He took her to a state of total ecstasy. They both had orgasms at the same time. After they finished she cleaned herself up first and put on another skimpy little nightie and then Ricky went into the bathroom with his clothes, cleaned himself up and got dressed.

She offered him something to eat and he said, "Nah, I have to go home. Vanessa is waiting for me."

A look of guilt came over that stink whore's face. She knew that what she was doing was going to hurt me deeply. She knew that I loved her as a sister, yet she still had sex with my man. I don't understand how she could do it. After everything we have been through over the years, didn't I mean anything to her? I would expect this from a man, but my best friend? Never! I swear the more I think about it now the more I feel like whipping her ass. But she couldn't help herself, or so she convinced herself. Ricky was so fine and sexy that she couldn't resist him, so she would tell me later. I guess I'm different. I don't give a damn how fine my friends' men are. I won't screw them. I have that much respect for my friends and myself. I'm sure a lot of you women that are reading this shit feel the same way I do. You would never have sex with your best friend's man. Would you? After all this time I had no idea that my friend Wanda was nothing more than a trailer trash. As for Ricky, he didn't give a damn about either one of us. Both of us were nothing more to him than pieces of ass.

We had been living in the apartment for only a few months before I noticed her. She was about twenty-four years old, somewhat pretty, with big breasts and an unusually big ass. If I had known what a bastard Ricky was I would have known that she was going to be trouble. As I passed by her she just looked at me with a stupid grin on her face and walked into her apartment. What a slut! I had to go away for a few days for a business seminar. My boss demanded that all the executives attend the conference. I didn't want to leave Ricky but I had no choice.

"I wish you could come with me," I said lovingly to Ricky.

"Honey you know I'd go with you if I could but the firm was just hired by a rather large company to handle a lawsuit filed recently against them," Ricky said innocently. "My firm needs me. It's crucial that I be here now. I love you and I'll miss you but I have obligations here. I just can't go bouncing off to a seminar just because your boss demands it. I have law partners who hold my balls in their hands. You know that one day I hope to make partner. This is the case that just might do it." He walked up behind me as I packed my clothing and wrapped his arms around me.

"Ricky we don't have time for this," I said as I pretended that I didn't want him. "I have to be at the airport in two hours."

Ricky whispered in my ear, "Just a few minutes is all I need." He turned me around, wrapped his arms around me and kissed me passionately. He walked me over to the bed and laid me down. He climbed on top of me and we quickly made love. He licked my breasts and sucked my nipples gently. He knew how much this turned me on. I didn't have much time so Ricky made love to me as fast as he could. He was able to take me to a state of total ecstasy in less than fifteen minutes. We both had orgasms at the same time. After we finished, Ricky stayed in bed and I went into the bathroom to wash up. I came out, got dressed and just at that moment I heard the taxi driver honk his horn.

"Ricky, the cab is here. I have to go honey. If I don't hurry I'm going to miss my flight." I rushed over to him and kissed him on the mouth.

"You better go honey. You don't want to miss your flight. I'm going to get myself cleaned up. You go on. I'll see you in a few days."

I grabbed my bags and ran out the apartment and headed for the airport.

Ricky picked up the phone, called the slut down the hall and said, "The bitch is gone. I'll leave the front door unlocked. You can come on over. Wear something sexy. I'll see you soon." He hung up the phone, went to the front door and unlocked it. He then went into the bathroom to take a shower. The tramp left her apartment, walked down the hall to my apartment, opened our front door and walked on in as though she owned the place. She was wearing only a thin night gown. She walked into our apartment and headed straight to our bedroom. She knew exactly where it was. Obviously she had been in there before. She took off her gown and dropped it to the floor. She walked into the bathroom and slithered her fat ass right into the shower with Ricky. They made love right in my shower. Ricky was acting like an eligible bachelor. He was being a scoundrel and a pig. After they finished she went into the bedroom with Ricky and laid her stink fat ass right in my bed. This slut was in my bed with her face on my pillow after just making love to my man in my shower where I bathe myself at. Let me ask you ladies a couple of questions. "Is this bitch crazy? Does she have a fucking death wish?" Ladies, what would you do if your sexy neighbor snuck into your home, slithered her fat ass into your shower where you wash your body up and made love to your man? What would you do if you found out that not only was she sleeping in your bed, but she actually put her head on the pillow that you slept on? What would you do if your man let her do this without giving it another thought?

As I boarded the plane that afternoon all I could think about was Ricky lying in bed all alone. A smile came on my face as I reminisced about us making love before I left the house. I smiled as the memory of our lovemaking before I left played over and over in my mind. I already missed Ricky. I missed his touch. I missed his smell. I missed him. As for Ricky, he really didn't give a damn.

I started becoming suspicious of Ricky's infidelities a few weeks after I got back from my business trip. Ricky and I had the same type of cell phones and we were always switching phones by mistake. One day I grabbed Ricky's phone off the kitchen counter thinking it was mine. I grabbed my attaché case and rushed out the door for work. I was stuck in rush hour traffic with my radio blasting. I was singing along to my favorite song. Ricky's phone rang and I answered it.

I turned the radio down low and asked, "This is Vanessa, who am I speaking with?"

A woman's voice on the other end said, "Who the hell is this answering Ricky's phone? Who is this?"

I said in my mean I'm gonna kick your ass bitch voice, "This is Vanessa, Ricky's woman. Why are you calling my man's cell phone? In fact, who the hell are you?"

"What do you mean Ricky's woman? He didn't tell me he had a woman. That bastard! You wait until I see him."

"Fuck all that," I said angrily. "Who are you, trick?"

"Who are you calling a trick?"

"I'm calling you a trick," I responded angrily.

"Obviously you don't have what it takes to hang on to your man or he wouldn't have been with me. Just tell Ricky to call me. Tell him it's his other woman."

Ladies, what would you do if another woman called you and told you that she was your man's other woman? She told me that Ricky and she worked for the same law firm. She was one of the paralegals in the firm and Ricky took her out a few times. He obviously didn't tell her that he already had a woman. She said her name was Tammy.

"Ricky is my man and he always will be," I yelled. "You may have had him but he came home to me. He didn't stay with your sorry ass. He knows where his home is and it ain't with you, trick!"

"You know what? You can have that two-timing son-of-a-bitch," she said angrily. "I don't need this shit. I refuse to have all this damn drama in my life. I'm done. He's nothing but leftovers and his sex wasn't that good anyway. He's nothing but a mini-dicked loser. Bye ho!" She hung up the phone.

I was furious. At that moment I wanted to kill Ricky. I went on to work anyway even though I felt like going to his law firm and kicking his ass in front of everybody. I was in a bad mood all day long and my girls were concerned about me. I didn't want my girls all up in my business so I told them that nothing was wrong. I worked for our advertising firm as an advertiser. It was my job to come up with ad campaigns for companies to draw in customers for their products. I was in charge of a new account and I needed to know if our legal consultant Wanda had some important legal documents signed by the CEO of the company that had hired us.

I called Wanda into my office and I asked, "Wanda did you have a chance to get those legal documents signed by Mr. Washington? I need them before I can get started on their campaign."

"They haven't been signed yet. I'm waiting for his lawyer to call me."

I was still angry at Ricky for cheating on me with the paralegal in his law firm and I began to take out my frustrations on everyone around me including her.

"Damn Wanda," I yelled. "What the fuck is taking you so long? It's your responsibility to get this shit done so that we can move along with the campaign. It doesn't take this long to get a contract signed. You need to move your ass before they change their minds and decide to go with a different advertising firm. You need to do your job. Isn't that what you were hired for?"

Wanda became angry. "Wait!" she yelled. "Hold on just a damn minute. I don't know what your problem is but don't take your frustrations out on me. I don't know who the hell you're talking to like that but you need to check yourself."

"I'm sorry Wanda," I said apologetically. "I'm just so pissed off right now. I didn't mean to take my frustrations out on you. This really has nothing to do with you. It's Ricky. I took his cell phone to work with me this morning and some bitch called. She said she was a paralegal at the law firm where he works. She claims that Ricky and she have been seeing each other behind my back and that they have been out a few times. The bitch said that they had sex. I swear if Ricky cheated on me I'm going to whip both their asses. I don't know who to believe or what to do. I love him so much and I refuse to lose him over some tramp."

I didn't know it but Wanda felt nauseous. She felt guilty for what she was doing to me and she felt like she was losing Ricky. If Ricky cheated it was not only on me, it was on her also. She knew that Ricky was sleeping with me but he had promised her that he would soon be leaving me for her. She had no idea that Ricky was sleeping with yet another woman.

"What's the matter honey?" I asked. "You look like you're about to throw up or something."

"No," she whispered. "Nothing is wrong. I'm just concerned about you. That's all."

She was obviously a selfish lying bitch, but I didn't know it at the time. She didn't give a damn about me or what I was going through. She only cared about herself.

"Don't worry about me," I said as a matter of factly. "I'll be fine. You know what? Forget it. I have work to do. I'm not going to spend my whole day worrying about this. The bitch is probably lying anyway. She's probably just a jealous colleague. I'll deal with this later when I talk to Ricky. That bastard has some explaining to do." I looked over at Wanda with concern. She didn't look well. "Honey, are you sure that you're alright? You look like you're about to faint."

"I'm alright. Nothing's wrong. I have to get back to my office. I'll see you later." She walked out of my office with a strange look on her face. I didn't know it at the time but that look was a combination of guilt and fear at the same time. She was guilty for deceiving me behind my back and scared of losing Ricky. After I got home that evening I was still very angry. I didn't fix anything for dinner. Ricky could starve to death and I wouldn't give a damn. When Ricky got home he walked into the kitchen and placed his briefcase on the counter. He looked around the kitchen and saw that nothing had been prepared for dinner.

"Hey, what's going on?" he asked. "I'm starving and nothing is ready for dinner. Are you planning on ordering something in? Oh by the way, we switched phones again this morning. You have my phone."

"Yeah I have your phone," I said angrily. "Oh by the way Tammy from your law firm called."

He was shocked that I even knew her name. "What?" he asked innocently. "Tammy? Who's Tammy?"

"The bitch you've been screwing at work. Don't play dumb with me Ricky because I swear I will kick your ass, you and that whore at work. Who the hell is Tammy and how did she get your cell phone number?"

Ricky walked slowly over to me and begged me to calm down. "Honey, you have it all wrong? Oh, I remember now. Tammy is one of the paralegals in my law firm. I gave her my cell phone number a few weeks ago because we were all working on a big case with one of our major clients. I needed her to do some legal research for me. Her research ran over long into the night and I gave her my cell phone number and told her to give me a call when all the research was complete. This case was important to my career and I didn't want to leave anything to chance."

"Oh, really?" I asked suspiciously. "She didn't tell me any of the bullshit you just told me. In fact, she said that the two of you went out on several dates and that you slept with her. Don't lie to me Ricky. Be a man and tell me honestly what the hell is going on. Are you cheating on me with other bitches?"

"Look honey. This girl has a crush on me. She has made it perfectly clear that she wants me. I have told her on more than one occasion that I have a woman and that I am not interested in her. Do you really think that I would cheat on you after everything we have meant to each other? Do you really think that I would leave a beautiful woman like you for a stink whore like that? To pay me back for turning her down I think she is trying to do everything she can to hurt me by breaking us up. I love you. I will never cheat on you or do anything to hurt you. Don't you know me by now? We have been through too much for me to throw our relationship away. I'm not a fool. I know what I got and I'm not going to do anything to destroy our relationship. I love you and I always will. You can trust me. Come here."

He sounded convincingly remorseful when in actuality he didn't give a damn. He walked up to me and looked right into my eyes with his big brown eyes. He placed his hands on the sides of my face and kissed me passionately. "Sweetheart, you have nothing to worry about," he said. "I'm your man, and only your man. Trust and believe in me. You are the only woman in my life."

He dismissed my accusations as being nothing more than my imagination. Damn. What a fucking liar! Ladies I ask you. Is your man as good a liar as mine was? Have you noticed that men have a way of lying that is so convincing that they actually start to believe their lies themselves? A man can look you straight in the eyes without flinching and lie to you so well that you start apologizing to him for doubting him in the first place. It's almost as though men go to a special lying school when they are young boys and train specifically on how to lie to their women when they grow up. They are experts at it! At that moment I had a choice. I could believe Ricky or believe that trick on his cell phone. Like most women I chose to believe my man even though all evidence pointed to the fact that he had slept with this girl. I can't believe I was so stupid. Ladies, why do we do this shit to ourselves? Why do we let men walk all over us like this? Why do we let them make such fools of us? I actually apologized to Ricky for doubting him. I kissed him and begged for his forgiveness. Ricky played his part to the last second. He actually made me feel guilty for accusing him of cheating. This bastard made a complete fool of me. After he finished making me apologize to him, even though he was cheating on me and made me feel like shit, he wanted me to give him a blow job.

"Come on," he whispered. "Do me. You know what I want. Show me how much you really love me." He unzipped his pants and I kneeled on the floor and did as he asked. I put his penis in my mouth and went to work. It's amazing the things I can do with my tongue. I know exactly how to please my man. I submitted to his wishes and advances out of fear of making him mad at me again. After I finished he had me fix him dinner after all. After he ate he went into his office and snorted some cocaine. Is this guy a fucking loser or what? Even after that incident there were other clues that Ricky was cheating on me. But, like other women I let him sweet-talk me into believing that it was just my imagination and that I was his one-and-only love when in fact, he was screwing every woman in sight. There was the time when I was doing his laundry and happened to smell one of his shirts. It had a cheap perfume smell to it that I obviously didn't use. Ricky's excuse was that during lunch hour one afternoon after he had lunch with a client downtown, he ran into an old female colleague of his and she gave him a hug. He said that it was all innocent and in fact, the client was right next to him at the time that the woman gave him a hug. I later found out that Ricky did indeed run into a colleague downtown, but that he was not with a client.

In fact, Ricky and this woman had actually dated in graduate school and had lived together for a short while. After they had lunch the two of them sleep together at a hotel downtown. Ricky never did make it back to work on that particular afternoon. Later that night he came home and made love to me. Ricky didn't know if this woman had AIDS, syphilis, gonorrhea or what. If she did then so could I. Women I want you all to understand something. Every woman your man sleeps with without a condom, hypothetically you just slept with her too. The DNA from her diseased vaginal juices could now be inside of you. Wake up ladies. If she has AIDS now so could you. Check your man before it's too late especially if you have children. Also, see a doctor immediately and get tested if you suspect your man has slept with another woman or several other women. You don't know if they used a condom or not. Your children don't need both of you to die! Have any of you ladies had a close friend or relative who contracted HIV from their husbands or boyfriends who were cheating on them?

There was the time that I found one of Ricky's shirts and he convinced me that the lipstick stain on the shirt was mine and accidentally rubbed off my lips when I was hugging him. The problem was that the color of the lipstick was two shades lighter than the red that I used. There was the time that I found an open condom wrapper on the floor of his SUV and he swore to me that it must have belonged to a friend of his. He stated that his best friend Mark used his SUV one Saturday night when I was away at a business seminar.

"Honey, I had nowhere to go that Saturday night when you weren't in town. Why would I want to go anywhere without my baby right next to my side? I just stayed home and dreamed about when my Vanessa was going to come home. Baby I missed you so much. I couldn't wait for you to come home. Antwain wanted to ride a lady in a luxury vehicle and we both know how fly mine is so I let him use it. He didn't want his woman to know that he was going out with another bitch. He is definitely cheating on his woman. Don't even worry about that shit. You are the lucky one. Your man is not cheating on you. You have nothing to worry about."

That was one of many occasions that Ricky was able to sweet talk me into believing his bullshit. His sweetness and fake compassion threw me completely off guard. I had no idea, but he was being extremely calculating and devious. I was being set up for more pain and humiliation. Ricky had emotionally abused me so badly that I didn't know what to believe anymore. I had always been good at judging character but, I couldn't trust my own instincts anymore.

There were the times that the phone at home would ring. I would pick up the phone and say, "Hello. Hello." No one would answer. They would just hang up the phone.

It was a few days before Valentine's Day. After work Ricky drove to a nearby florist. He walked in and said to the florist, "Hello, how's it going? Hey man I need to order some flowers."

"For your wife or girlfriend?" the florist asked.

"They're for my woman, yes, and a few close friends. Let's just leave it at that. Let me have a dozen roses and have them sent to my woman Vanessa. Give me another dozen of red roses for a friend of mine. Her name is Wanda. Also send a dozen roses to Brenda, Valerie, Tanya, and Ana."

"Ok my friend. I see you want to make a lot of ladies happy this Valentine. I'll have them delivered first thing Tuesday morning on Valentine's Day. How about that my friend?"

"Thank you my man. Here's a little bonus for you." Ricky gave him a tip and left the store with a couple dozen roses in his hands. He said that they were a pre-Valentines Day present for me. He also said, "Don't worry baby. There is more to come."

On Valentine's Day the following Tuesday I received another beautiful bouquet of flowers that was delivered right to my office. A few of the girls received flowers in the office that day from their men including my so-called friend Wanda. I asked sarcastically, "Wanda, you've been seeing a new guy? You sneaky ho! Who's your new man? Anyone I know?"

Wanda looked at me with what I didn't realize at the time was a guilty expression on her face."No," she said nervously. "No, Vanessa he isn't anyone you know. It's just some sweet guy who has a crush on me. I might go out with him, but I don't know. We'll see. I have to go. We'll talk later." She picked up her dozen roses from the receptionist's desk and hurried back to her office.

The receptionist Angelina said, "Vanessa those sure are some beautiful roses. Your man must love you a whole lot."

"Yes. Yes he does," I said proudly. "Thank you." I couldn't believe that a man like Ricky loved and respected me so much. I felt like his one and only true love and I knew that someday he was going to ask me to marry him. I smelled my roses as I walked back to my office while gently cradling them in my arms. I really loved Ricky. But, as for Ricky he really didn't give a damn.

Even though I got beautiful roses from Ricky that Valentine's Day it was the day that things turned for the worst for Ricky and me. I rushed home from work that afternoon to get things ready for our Valentine's Day dinner. I wanted everything to be perfect for our romantic evening together. I walked into the apartment and went into the kitchen. I grabbed a beautiful crystal vase and filled it half way with water. I placed my beautiful roses into the vase and placed the entire thing on the dining room table. I went back into the kitchen to prepare dinner. The night before I had seasoned down a pot roast and placed it in the refrigerator so that the seasoning could go all through it. Ladies, you know what I'm talking about. I took the roast out of the refrigerator and placed it in the oven to cook. I made Spanish rice, baby green peas, and buttered garlic rolls. I took out a bottle of champagne and placed it in a wine bucket full of ice to chill. The enticing smell from the meal spread throughout the entire house. After I finished preparing dinner, it was time for me to get sexy for my man. I went into the bedroom and pulled out a sexy, hot nightie and laid it on the bed. I didn't get any panties because I knew that on a night like that I wouldn't need them. I went into the shower and freshened myself up. I put some silky lotion all over my arms and legs. I slipped into my sexy nightie. I sat down in front of the vanity table and fixed my hair and makeup. I even did my nails. I was looking good and I knew Ricky wouldn't be able to resist me. I went back into the kitchen and grabbed some of our best china and set the dining room table. I lit the candles that were sitting on the dining room table and turned the lights down low. I went into the kitchen and turned off the food. I placed the food in beautiful serving dishes and carried them one by one to the dining room table. Everything looked beautiful. The only thing was missing was Ricky. It was getting late and I knew he would be home soon. I poured myself a small glass of white wine, sat down and waited for my man to walk through the door. The bastard never showed up. Ladies, what would you do if you spent hours of your time preparing for a romantic evening with your boyfriend, fiancé, or husband and he didn't bother to show up or even call you?

Ricky had a large bouquet of roses in his arms. He walked up to the door and rang the bell. The door opened and my other so-called best friend Barbara stood in the doorway. "Happy Valentine's Day baby," Ricky said. "These flowers are for you." Barbara smiled and gently took the flowers from Ricky.

"Thank you baby," she said. "Come on in. I've been waiting for you."

Ricky walked up to her and kissed her on the mouth. He kissed her so deeply and passionately you would have thought that he was going to suck her lips right down his throat. He walked into the apartment. She closed the front door behind him.

"Damn girl," Ricky said. "It smells good in here. What did you cook?"

"Are you hungry baby?" she asked. "Well, come right this way and let mama take care of you. I made you a delicious Valentine's Day dinner."

She led Ricky to her dining room where she had a romantic dinner prepared just for the two of them. She even had wine chilling in a wine cooler and lit candles illuminated the room. She poured a couple of glasses of wine and she and Ricky toasted to the evening. They ate dinner, laughed and talked. She stood up from her chair and walked around the table to Ricky. He opened his legs as she stood in between them. She put her arms around his neck and he wrapped his arms around her legs. Ricky kissed Barbara's belly. She got turned on and they kissed each other passionately on the lips.

Meanwhile, I was sitting at my dining room table alone waiting for Ricky to come home. After two hours I gave up. I fixed myself a plate of food and heated it in the microwave. I opened up the champagne and poured myself a drink. I ate dinner alone on Valentine's Day while my man spent the evening with one of my best friends. I drank almost a half bottle of champagne all by myself and went to bed alone. Back at Barbara's apartment, they had finished dinner and were in bed together. Ricky kissed Barbara on her neck. She closed her eyes and moaned as he placed his hand underneath her dress. He made love to her and after they finished he held her.

"Barbara I have to go home," he said. "Vanessa will be wondering where I am."

"What are you going to tell her? I'm sure she expected to have dinner with you tonight. She must be pissed by now. Ricky when are you going to tell her about us? We can't keep doing this. It's getting harder and harder for me to look her in the face. You need to leave her." Ladies, what would you do if you found out that more than one of your best friends was sleeping with your man behind your back and then smiling in your face when you saw them?

"It won't be long honey. I promise I'll tell her as soon as the time is right. Let me worry about all this. Don't worry your pretty little self. Daddy has it under control. Vanessa doesn't run things. I do. I'm the man and she'll do what the fuck I say." Ricky got out of Barbara's bed and took a shower. He kissed her once again and said goodbye to her. He left her apartment and headed for home. When Ricky finally arrived home I was passed out on the bed. He came into the bedroom and woke me up. I was groggy and in a very bad mood. The evening was ruined and I didn't want to hear any excuses from Ricky.

"Honey I'm sorry I'm late," he said. "I know how pissed off you are. Let me explain what happened. I had to work late. My boss called an emergency meeting for all the lawyers in the firm to discuss strategies on the big case we are working on. The company that has just acquired our services has just been hit with a multi-million dollar lawsuit and they need our help. No one was allowed to leave until the meeting was over. My boss didn't even want us using our cell phones unless it was a matter of life or death. Please, tell me you understand. I love you."

I was becoming less and less susceptible to his lies. I looked at Ricky and at that moment I wanted to kill him. "Do you have any idea the trouble I went through to make this a special evening for the two of us," I asked. "It's

Valentine's Day. It comes only once a damn year and you can't make an effort to be with me. I don't give a damn what your boss says. And I know you don't expect me to believe the bullshit story you just told me. Do I look that stupid? I know you spent the evening with some whore instead of with me."

Ricky tried to do what he usually did. He tried to make the failure of the evening my fault. "How can you get mad like this?" he yelled. "You know how important it is for me to make partner and this is the case that just might do it. Why are you always acting like a selfish bitch? I bust my ass day in and day out to make a better life for both of us and this is the thanks I get? What the hell is the matter with you Vanessa?" He was speaking to me unapologetically. I wanted to punch him in the face right then and there.

"Oh no," I yelled. "You are not going to blame this shit on me. I spent the entire day preparing for this holiday. I wanted to make you happy tonight. I did all of this to please your stupid ass. I didn't do it because I'm a selfish bitch."

"What did you say to me?" he asked. "Who do you think you're talking to like that? You don't disrespect me like that. Who the hell do you think you're talking to?"

"I'm talking to you, you stupid bastard!" I yelled.

"Obviously you're drunk from all that damn champagne you drank so I'm just gonna ignore your dumb ass right now. I'm gonna give you time to sober up and calm the fuck down. I'm gonna sleep in my office tonight. Stay away from me until you get your shit together. I have to come home to this after a long day at work? I don't need this shit." He grabbed a pillow and started walking toward his office. I stumbled up to him and grabbed his arm.

"Ricky please don't go," I cried. "I love you. Why are you doing these things to me? Why are you trying to hurt us? Don't you love me? Ricky!"

Ricky pushed me off of him and yelled, "Get off of me. Go to bed and sober up. Shit!" He walked into the office and slammed the door and locked it. I started screaming at Ricky to come out of his office.

I yelled, "Ricky, don't you dare walk away from me like this. Why don't you be a man and let's deal with this shit tonight?" I started banging on the office door but Ricky just ignored me. Banging on the door was actually giving me a headache. It was irritating me more than it was irritating Ricky. I gave up and went back to bed.

Ricky was locked up in his office. He did what he usually did. He pulled out some of his cocaine and poured a small line of it on his desk. He put one finger up to his nostril and snorted it with the other. He closed his eyes as the cocaine traveled through his bloodstream taking him to a state of total ecstasy. He passed out right in his office. The next morning I woke up and went into the kitchen to make some fresh coffee. I had a hangover and a splitting headache.

Ricky came out of the office and said, "Good morning." I just ignore him. "So you can't speak?" he asked. "You still have an attitude problem? You still want to act like a bitch? The hell with you then." He walked into the bathroom to get ready for work. I fixed myself a toasted bagel and ate it with a cup of coffee.

Ricky came out and asked, "Did you fix me something for breakfast or am I just suppose to starve?"

"You have two fucking hands," I said angrily. "Fix yourself some breakfast. I'm not your damn servant."

"You know what, the hell with this," he yelled in frustration. "I don't need this shit." He got his briefcase, walked out of the apartment and slammed the front door.

"Shit!" I whispered to myself. I went on to work. That night I waited for Ricky to come home so we could talk things out. Again he didn't come home. This time he stayed out all night long. He didn't even bother to call me to tell me where he was staying or that he was ok. He had never stayed out all night long before. I felt like things were really falling apart between us. I didn't know what to do. Ricky knocked on the front door of the apartment. The door opened and a woman stood in the doorway. It was my third so-called best friend Charlotte. She was the one who slept around a lot and felt that she didn't need to apologize to anyone for it. She said that what she did with her body was her damn business and everyone else could just kiss her ass.

"Ricky honey, what are you doing here at this time?" Charlotte asked. "I wasn't expecting you but I'm glad you came. What about Vanessa? Shouldn't you be going home to Vanessa? Won't she be looking for you? It's the evening after Valentine's."

Ricky walked into the apartment and Charlotte closed the front door as she followed him inside. Ricky laid his briefcase on the counter and loosened his tie. He sat down on the couch and put his head back. He was exhausted.

"What's the matter honey?"

"Ah shit," he said. "Vanessa and I had a big blow out last night and again this morning. That bitch is starting to get on my fucking nerves. Can I crash here with you tonight? I don't feel like going home and dealing with her shit."

"Of course baby," she replied happily. "You can stay here with me as long as you want. In fact, you can move in here with me if you want to. Wouldn't that be nice? I'd love it if you would leave Vanessa and move in here with me. Why don't you just leave her? She can never satisfy you the way that I can."

"I'm not leaving Vanessa for your trifling ass. I just need a break from her for one night. That's it. Don't get any other fucking ideas in that pretty little head of yours. In fact, don't try to think at all. I'll do the thinking for both of us."

"You don't have to talk to me in such an ugly way," Charlotte said with disappointment. He had hurt her feelings. "I was just asking. I love you and I'll do anything for you. What can I do for you?"

"Do you have anything up in here to eat? I'm hungry."

"Of course," she responded. "Let me fix you something right now. Just relax baby and unwind. Vanessa has got you all uptight." She went into the kitchen and fixed Ricky some dinner. Ricky took the remote control and clicked the television on to watch some news. He needed to unwind from a stressful day. Charlotte prepared their dinner and brought it to the dining table. They sat down and enjoyed the meal together as a couple. Ricky forgot about me. On that particular night she was his woman. I didn't matter to him at all. He really didn't give a shit! After they ate, my man took a shower in her apartment. She walked into the bathroom just as he was getting out of the shower. He started to dry his naked body off. She was turned on by how large he was.

"Can I get you something else?" she asked as she stared at his penis and his ass. Ricky knew that she was turned on and it pleased him. He pulled her up to him. He started rubbing her ass. He pulled her underwear off of her and kissed her. He led her into the bedroom, laid her on the bed and climbed on top of her. The two of them made love. They kissed, caressed and she moaned as he thrust himself into her. After they finished Ricky sat up and poured a small line of cocaine onto the side table. He covered his left nostril with one finger and snorted up the cocaine into his right nostril. He closed his eyes as the cocaine traveled throughout his body taking him to a state of total ecstasy. Charlotte turned over in bed and asked, "Can I try some?"

Ricky yelled angrily, "If I ever catch you messing with this shit that'll be it for us. I'll dump your trifling ass. I don't want a coke head for a bitch. Do you hear me?"

"Yeah," she pleaded. "Don't get mad with me baby. I was just asking. Damn. Calm down. Shit."

He asked angrily, "Why don't you get your ass up and go in the kitchen and fix me a snack? I'm hungry."

Charlotte got out of bed and put a robe on. She was terrified of angering him so she did as she was ordered to. She went into the kitchen and fixed him a turkey sandwich and got him a can of soda. She brought the food into the bedroom.

Ricky looked at what Charlotte had bought him and asked, "What the hell is this? You expect me to eat it like this? Charlotte, go back into the damn kitchen and put some mustard on the bread. Don't give me this regular white bread either. Put everything on a warmed roll and put the soda in a damn glass with some ice. You can't be this stupid." He was still high from the cocaine and his attitude was getting worse. He was easily annoyed by her and everything she did. He was quickly becoming out of control and unpredictable.

"You don't have to have such an ugly attitude and talk to me like that Ricky. You can ask me nicely."

"What did you just say to me? What did you say? You want me to ask you nicely bitch? Ok. I'll give you nice."

Ricky took his hand and slapped Charlotte so hard that she fell against the wall and landed on the floor. He grabbed her with one hand and then beat her with his fist. She screamed as he beat her over and over. Her screams went on deaf ears. He really didn't give a damn. The more she screamed, the more he beat her. It was giving him pleasure causing her pain. She had a busted lip, a black eye and black and blue marks on her face and neck. Ricky beat her because he wanted her to know who the man was. He beat her because he was high and simply because he could. Charlotte began to cry hysterically. She was bleeding from the corner of her mouth. Every part of her body hurt. Ricky pulled her up onto her feet. She tried to wrap her arms around his neck and kiss him. He wasn't interested.

She whispered, "Why do you treat me this way Ricky? You know I love you baby. I'll do anything for you. I can make you happy baby. What do you want me to do for you? Just tell me baby." Ricky pushed Charlotte off of him.

"Get off of me. Go fix me something to eat like I said. Don't piss me off again."

She went into the bathroom took a napkin and washed the blood off of her face. Charlotte was still crying as she went into the kitchen and fixed Ricky's food the way he asked. He walked back into the living room, sat on the couch and turned the television back on.

The next night Ricky finally left her place and came back home. He walked into the apartment and said, "Hello Vanessa."

"Where did you stay last night and all day? I was worried about you. I didn't know what had happened to you. I didn't know if you were hurt or in trouble and needed me. Why didn't you call me or answer any of my phone calls. I called you several times and got no answer. I left several messages for you to call me back but you never did. Where were you?"

"I stayed at my boy's house last night. We were just chilling. Don't get all bent out of shape. I didn't want to get into another argument with you. I needed to clear my head. That's all."

"Are you hungry? Did you eat anything? Can I fix you a snack?"

"No." He walked into his office and slammed the door. I left him alone that night because I wasn't in the mood to argue with him. The next morning I got up early and fixed Ricky some breakfast. I wanted to show him that I still loved him and was willing to serve my man. I wanted him to know that I was still his woman. I made him his favorite breakfast. I made him some toast, eggs, and sausage. I also made him a fresh cup of coffee and some fresh squeezed orange juice. He came out to the kitchen and grabbed the cup of coffee. He took a few sips and grabbed his briefcase to head out for work. My hard work fixing him breakfast just the way he liked it meant nothing to him. He really didn't give a damn.

"Aren't you hungry? I made a good breakfast for you. Aren't you going to eat this morning?"

"No. I don't have time. I have to go. I'll see you later. You eat it or just throw the shit away." He walked out of the apartment. I was so hurt and disappointed. I couldn't believe he was acting so callous and non-caring. What a bastard! I took his breakfast and threw it in the garbage.

I yelled out, "Fuck you then!"

I too headed out to work. I had a lousy day and was in a really bad mood all day. I needed to unwind. I didn't want to go home and deal with Ricky's bullshit. Besides, there were many evenings that he went out to the clubs to unwind and get away from me. It was my turn. I met with my so-called girlfriends for a girl's night out later that evening. We met at the same club where we had first met Ricky. I wanted to have a few drinks and wind down. I didn't know it at the time but all three bitches were about to destroy my world. They had all unknowingly decided to tell me that they were in love with my man at the same time. My entire world was about to be destroyed. We met up at the club at about the same time and went to a table. We ordered drinks from the bartender. The ladies were unusually quiet that evening and I couldn't understand why. Charlotte wasn't talking a lot of bullshit about men the way that she usually did. Wanda wasn't acting like a big mouthed bitch like she usually did. Barbara wasn't acting like her usual conceited self. She wasn't flaunting her accomplishments the way she usually did. Nor was she making sarcastic cracks at the other girls.

"What the hell is going on?" I asked myself. I thought I had problems with Ricky's ass. I didn't understand why the girls were acting so distant and so cold. They were my girls. They were like sisters to me. I loved them and they weren't even acting right. I didn't understand what was happening. I finally came out and said, "Ok bitches! What's the problem? Why is everyone so quiet tonight? This is supposed to be girls' night out. The three of you have never been this damn quiet before in your whole fucking lives. What's up?" I didn't know it at that moment but the three of them were about to contribute to the subsequent breakup of my relationship with Ricky. The three of them just looked at each other with stupid expressions on their face.

"Charlotte, why are you wearing those stupid big sunglasses inside of a dark nightclub?" I asked. "Have you lost your damn mind? Who do you think you are a fucking Hollywood actress or something? Take those damn things off. You don't need to wear them in here. You look ridiculous."

Charlotte said angrily, "Don't worry about what I'm wearing Vanessa. Mind your own damn business."

I was surprised that she was acting so stink. "Well excuse the hell out of me," I said angrily.

Wanda reached over and snatched the sunglasses off. Charlotte had bruises on her face and a blackened eye from the ass beating that Ricky had given her.

"Charlotte what the hell happened to you?" I asked with concern. "Who did that to you honey?"

Charlotte lowered her head in shame. You could see the embarrassment on her face. She didn't know how to tell us that the man she loved, who happened to be Ricky, had beaten her so badly. Without thinking, she started to lie to us.

"I met a guy and he got a little rough with me. It's nothing. Don't worry about it."

"Don't worry about it?" Barbara asked with confusion. "Don't worry about it? What the hell is the matter with you? Are you crazy bitch? Some man beats you like that and you don't want us to worry about it? That doesn't make any sense. Did you call the police?"

I touched Charlotte's cheek gently and said, "Let me see that. Oh god, look what that bastard did to you." I looked at the bruises on her face. "Does it hurt? Who is this guy anyway? Is it someone any of us knows?"

"Well, no," Charlotte said unconvincingly. "It's nobody that any of you know." We could all hear the uneasiness in her voice.

"I could never let any man hit me like that," I responded with pride. "I have too much respect for myself to let a man abuse me like that. Ricky isn't perfect but he would never hit a woman like that. Damn. Seeing what has happened to you makes me appreciate being with Ricky even more. There are women all over the world being beaten by their men right now as we speak. Every minute of every day a woman is being abused by someone. That's fucked up! I feel so lucky that Ricky is my man. I know we have our problems but he loves me and only me. He respects me. Ricky is my man and I intend to make things work. I'm going to fight to keep our relationship going. I know that man loves me and would do anything for me. Charlotte I'm sorry this happened to you. Why don't you change your mind and see a doctor? Your injuries could be worse than you imagined. What if something is broken? Do you need me to take you to the hospital? Bitch I know you're not stupid enough to see this man again. If you ever see that abusive bastard again I personally will beat your ass myself."

Wanda with the big mouth came out and said, "Ok, I have something to say. This is bullshit! I can't take listening to you say how much Ricky loves you and how much you are going to work to make your relationship work. You have no relationship with Ricky. I can't believe you're so stupid you haven't figured this shit out yet. There is no easy way to say this. No matter what way I say this you are going to be hurt Vanessa. I have to do this right now because you are deluding yourself into thinking that Ricky actually loves you. I'm just gonna come right out and say it. You know I love you Vanessa but, Ricky and I have been seeing each other and I love him. He is not your man. He is mine. I know he loves me and wants to be with me."

Ladies, what if your best friend came up to you and told you that she was in love with your man and he wanted to be with her and not you? Would you give her a hug or whip her ass?

I was mortified. All this time I had been struggling to align my feelings with the perception that he was cheating on me. I refused to believe it. I blocked the undeniable evidence right out of my mind even though it was staring me right in the face. I had been terrified that I would lose him and because of my bitch-assed friend I just did. "What did you just say to me bitch?" I asked in total shock. "You've been seeing who? Ricky! What the hell are you talking about? Ricky's my man."

"No. He's my man," my friend Wanda yelled out.

"You're supposed to be my best friend Wanda. You're nothing more than a stick ass whore! You're such a stink-ass bitch! How could you do this to me? What the hell were you thinking? What about our friendship? Don't I mean anything to you? How could you stab me in the back like this? I don't understand you. I don't understand you at all."

"Wait a damn minute!" Charlotte yelled. "What do you mean you've been seeing Ricky and that he's your man? Ricky is my man Wanda. We've been seeing each other for weeks now and he told me that he loves me. I don't know what the hell you're talking about."

Barbara began to cry unexpectedly. We thought that she was crying because we were hurting each other emotionally and she felt sorry for the breakdown of our relationship. None of us could ever imagine that she too was the cause of the end of our friendship.

"What the hell are you crying about Barbara?" I asked. "This doesn't have a damn thing to do with you. This is between me and these two bitches over here."

"Ricky and I have been seeing each other for about a month now and I am in love with him," she whispered softly with fear in her voice. She feared that I would jump up and whip her ass. Believe me. The thought did cross my mind. "I'm so sorry Vanessa. I didn't mean for you to find out like this. I don't know what happened. Ricky came over one night and it just happened. Charlotte, did Ricky beat you? Was it him?"

Because they were my friends I could never have dreamed that there would be any impropriety between them and Ricky. My heart ached. I was broken-hearted.

"What do you mean it just happened? What happened bitch? What is 'it'? What the hell are you talking about? What? Did Ricky trip and his dick just fell into your mouth?" I screamed.

By this time, everyone in the entire club had heard what was going on and was all fascinated. They were giggling and laughing behind our backs. This was better than a soap-opera to them. The four of us started screaming at each other. We called each other bitches, whores, and sluts. The entire club was looking at us. Some of them hurried out of the club in fear that we would start fighting or maybe even pull out guns and start firing. Finally the manager of the club came over with a couple of bouncers and asked us to leave his club. The bouncers stood in front of us like a couple of gorillas ready to pounce on us at any second and beat our asses.

"Ladies, I can't have this kind of thing in my club," the manager said in a fake ass Italian accent. He was trying to sound like a gangster when in fact he sounded like a fool. "You four are disturbing my other patrons so I'm going to have to ask all four of you to leave right now. Get the hell out of here. If you don't leave now, I'm going to call the police. Don't any of you ever come back in here again. None of you are welcome in here. If any of you ever show up here again I will have my men here personally beat all of your asses. By the time we're done with you none of your boyfriends will be able to recognize your faces. Am I making myself clear? Are you hearing me bitches? Get the fuck out of here."

The four of us got up to leave the club and as we did, we were still cursing each other out. The manager of the club shook his head at us as we were leaving. He couldn't believe how ignorant and stupid we were acting. Everyone in the club was still staring at us. We were so mad that we didn't even notice. When we got outside we continued to yell at each other. It was like one big bitch fest. Wanda with her big mouth kept talking a lot of shit. I was pissed off already and she made things worst. I couldn't take her bullshit anymore. I walked up to her and punched her in the face. You would have thought that I was a professonal boxer or something. I then began to whip her ass. The other two girls tried to break us up.

"Stop it dammit!" Barbara cried. "If we don't get out of here the manager is going to call the police. Do you want to go to jail tonight over this damn man? He's not worth it. Stop it!"

I hated to admit it but Barbara was right so we broke the fight up. All of us realized that Ricky was nothing more than a piece of shit. He wasn't worth us getting arrested over. Ladies, this is what we do. Instead of being mad at the man and kicking his ass, we turn on each other. We need to stick together as sisters and women and love and support one another. We need to stand together and lift each other up when men dog us out and hurt us the way that they do. We are sisters. We are as one. Wait a minute. You know what? Forget all that sister shit! I'm not trying to be this bitch's sister. I took my fist and punched Wanda in the face again and knocked that trifling bitch to the ground. Come on ladies. Don't judge me. What would you do if you found out that your best friend was having sex with your man? She fell to the ground and blood dripped from her broken tooth. I told all three of them to kiss my ass and that I hated them and I didn't want to have anything to do with them ever again. Bitches!

I cried all the way home. I was so hurt that I didn't know what to do. I felt physically ill and thought for a second that I was going to vomit. I had been betrayed by not only the man I loved, but by all three of my best friends. I felt humiliated on so many different levels. The four of us were just like sisters. I didn't have a sister so I embraced the three of them as my sisters. I loved them. They were my family. We shared more than a lifetime together. We shared our deepest secrets. We knew each other's thoughts. We could finish each other's sentences. We knew what the other was going to say even before she said a word. We cried together. We hurt together. We knew how to build each other up when we were down and how to celebrate together when we were all up. Now, it was over. No longer would we hang out at each other's home like little girls except that we would get drunk and talk about men and sex. No longer would we go out and get so drunk that we had to hold each others hair up while we vomited in the streets. No longer would we tease men and find ways to embarrass them for our own amusement. No longer would we call each other bitches and whores out of endearment not out of disrespect. If another woman called us a bitch or a whore we would beat their asses not each other. I lost my sisters. I lost not only my best friends but my confidantes. I also lost my man. I finally awakened from the illusion that I created in my own mind that Ricky was in love with me. I felt like I had just lost everything. I was so hurt and confused. My heart ached and I didn't know how to make it stop. On top of all of that I had to go home and deal with Ricky. I had to confront him and let him know that now I knew. I knew that he had fucked my friends. I knew that he had fucked the women at his firm. I knew that he had slept with the neighbor. I knew that there were probably more women around the city that he had been with. I knew. When I arrived home it was dark in the apartment and very quiet. I thought that Ricky must have gone out with a few of his boys. I placed my keys and purse on the counter and walked to the bedroom to get undressed and put on something more comfortable.

When I got to the bedroom I turned on the light and couldn't believe what I saw. I was exasperated by what I was seeing. Ricky was in our bed with the slut who lived down the hall from us. Ricky was on top of her and they were making love. I closed my eyes for a second. I became nauseas and thought that I was going to throw up. I struggled to catch my breath. I felt breathless. I stared at him in amazement at his gall. The emotional pain I felt was indescribable. Ricky jumped out of the bed and grabbed his pants off of the dresser and stumbled as he quickly put them on.

As he put his pants on he yelled, "Oh shit! Vanessa, what are you doing here baby? I thought you were going out." He made a mediocre attempt at appeasing me.

He said unconvincingly, "Honey it's not what you think. We weren't doing anything. I love you and only you. She was visiting and felt faint so I invited her to lie down for a minute. I was just trying to comfort her and make sure that she was okay. This is all innocent."

His attempt at twisting my mind and convincing me that I was hallucinating wasn't working this time. The woman in my bed jumped up and started to put her clothes on. I was blocking the doorway so there was no way for her to escape my ass whipping. Now I ask you women of the world. If you came home and found your man in your bed having sex with another woman what would you do? I know damn well you wouldn't offer her a cup of tea and some cupcakes. I walked over to the bitch and tried to slap the shit out of her. I grabbed her by the hair and tried to snatch her hair weave out. She had a weave that was over two months old and looked like shit anyway. I was doing the bitch a favor. She was terrified. She started screaming and was trying to fight me off of her.

"I'm sorry. I'm sorry," she cried out. "Please don't do this. Please. Ricky, help me!" I punched her in the face so hard she fell to the floor. I took my fist and started punching her in the face.

"Oh shit!" Ricky shouted. He jumped over the bed to where we were at and pulled me off of her. He held me back as the girl grabbed the rest of her things and ran out of the apartment. She was a hot mess. Her hair was all over her head and some of it was lying on my bedroom floor. Her clothes were all ripped up and had her blood on them from my ass-whipping. Ricky continued to restrain me as I started screaming at him to let me go. One of my arms got loose and I reached up and scratched Ricky in the face. I felt my long fingernails piercing his flesh. Ricky threw me on the bed and held me down. "Calm the fuck down Vanessa. Calm down."

"The hell with you Ricky!" I screamed. "The hell with you. I found out tonight that you have been screwing all three of my best friends and now I have to come home and find you screwing that bitch down the hall. I will never forgive you for this Ricky. Never!" I felt like my heart had just shattered. I started crying and Ricky released my arms. You could tell he was tired from holding me down. He was breathing heavily and trying to catch his breath.

"What the hell are you talking about?" he asked guiltily. "You think that I was sleeping with all three of your friends? What friends?"

"Wanda, Barbara and Charlotte told me tonight that you are sleeping with all three of them. They admitted everything to me. Did you beat Charlotte? You're not only a cheater but you beat on women too? Who the hell are you? I don't even know who or what the fuck you are? If you beat her like that then your ass needs to go to jail. If I find out that it was you I will personally call the police myself. You know what, I can't take this shit anymore. Don't say another word to me Ricky. Just get your shit and get the hell out of this apartment. You're not welcome here anymore. Get out!"

"You know what, I don't need this shit and I don't need you. You're nothing but a trifling bitch anyway. If you knew how to fuck a man I wouldn't have to go in the streets for other bitches. All of this is your fault. I can't help it if you don't know how to please a man."

So now it was my fault that he was cheating on me. This man actually tried to convince me that I wasn't enough of a woman to keep him happy when in actuality no woman on the face of the earth was good enough for him in his mind.

"Get the fuck out of here Ricky. Now!"

Ricky quickly grabbed a bag, threw a few things in it and hurried out of the apartment. As he was leaving he said, "I'll pick up the rest of my things when your stupid ass is not home. Goodbye Vanessa."

I fell to my knees. I cried harder than I ever had before. I lost Ricky and all three of my best friends in one night. I was devastated. As for Ricky, he really didn't give a damn. Even though I still loved him I never spoke to Ricky again. Nor did I speak to Charlotte, Barbara or Wanda. The last I heard, Ricky was living with Charlotte and was occasionally still beating her ass and she was too stupid to leave him. He was cheating behind her back with Barbara and Wanda. I guess dogs will never change. As for me, I eventually got over Ricky but it was a long time before I trusted another man or woman. I pulled out my bible and began reading it again. I attended church regularly and asked God to forgive me for my sins. I got my self-respect back and realized that I was still a child of God in Heaven. I had become a woman toughened by betrayal and humiliation. I became strong. I was whole again.

Chapter 3

I'M WRITING THIS letter to all my sisters around the world who have been with a physically abusive alcoholic. I understand exactly what you're going through. Ladies, it's not your fault. My man Anthony almost killed me and my son. The father of my child left me and my son all alone in Miami, Florida. When my new man and I first met he showed no signs of a propensity for violence. That is, he showed no propensity for violence in my mind. But as for my friends and family, they saw something else. They saw a violent man. They could sense his rage. They didn't trust him at all. They were afraid of him. Everyone told me to get away from him before he killed me, but I stayed. I stayed for so long and put up with so much of his bullshit. He tore down my self-esteem until I felt that I was lower than a dog. Hell, even dogs got better treatment than I did. After he tore my self-esteem down he beat me over and over again. His behavior was contradictory and confused in that he would tell me he loved me and then beat on me at the same time. It was as though he had a split personality. He caused me to lose myself. I felt like I was nothing. I could literally feel my spirit leaving me with every punch and slap that he gave me. I died inside. I felt like I was not good enough for any man. I know that there are thousands of women all over the world who feel the same way. What was wrong with me I told myself? How could I allow myself to be physically abused like this?

There are ladies out there who know exactly what I'm talking about. I loved Anthony and I would do anything to please him. I gave and gave into the relationship but Anthony gave nothing. What an evil bastard he was. I must have been the stupidest woman on earth. No other woman could have been that dumb. I lost faith in myself and in men. I would never put my trust or my life in the hands of a man ever again. The first time that he hit me he begged for my forgiveness and then promised me that it would never happen again. I believed him. And besides, everyone is entitled to one mistake, aren't they? If a man hits you once and promises not to ever do it again that's ok. Am I right ladies? I told myself that it was my fault for making him so mad and causing him to hit me. Ladies please do not be my judge and jury. I am not the only one. There are millions of women all over the world just like me. I am not the only one. I know he loved me and would never hit me unless I had done something to provoke him, so it must have been my fault. Right? Oh God, what am I saying? Listen ladies, it's never ok for a man to hit you. I don't give a damn how mad he gets. No man ever has the right to hit you.

I got to the point where I couldn't take it any more. I reached deep within my soul and got the strength I needed to save myself and my son. I got strong, not only for myself, but for my child as well. I decided to put my safety and that of my child first. No man is worth risking my son's life for. My son is my inspiration. I had no right in bringing that kind of danger and evil into my son's life. I realize that now. I had to put an end to this if we were going to survive. I had to leave my man. I embraced my womanhood and my motherhood. I was whole again. I no longer felt fragmented. I picked up my bible and prayed for God to give me strength. It had been such a long time since I read my bible. Ladies, pick up your bibles again and pray. Ask Jesus for forgiveness and allow the Holy Spirit of God to come into your life again and give you guidance. Allow a mighty God to put your spirit at peace. Trust in him again. He has always loved you and no matter what has happened to you he always will. It doesn't matter if you honored him in the past and then walked away from him or if you never knew him at all. He forgives. He always forgives. I dug deep within my soul and realized that God had given me strength to protect not only myself, but my child as well. I learned the hard way that my child had to come first before a man. My child became my main focus in life. Having a man came last. I did everything I could to please Anthony, but he was never satisfied. I was not enough for him. He wanted more. But, he wanted more of what? I don't think even Anthony knew exactly what the hell he wanted. I realize now that I wasn't the problem. Anthony was the problem. He was an alcoholic and a physically abusive man.

He destroyed us. It wasn't my fault. He was sick. He needed help. Ladies, please do not judge me for staying with him for as long as I did and putting up with his physical abuse. I am not alone. There are millions of women all over the world just like me. We are the same. We are as one.

———

My name is Michelle Weber and I'm a twenty-nine year old single mother with one child. We live in Miami, Florida. I have a twelve year old son. He is a bright child but he is going through a stage when he is sarcastic all the time and a know-it-all. Moms you know exactly what I'm talking about. You know the phase when a child reaches that annoying age when he begins not to listen to what you have to say and thinks that you are the meanest woman on the entire planet and you don't know what you're talking about. He was going through that tender age when he thought that he knew everything. But, he was a good kid who studied hard and never got into trouble; that is not until Anthony came into our lives. Before Anthony came, my twelve year old son considered himself to be the man of the house, the only man in my life and wasn't too keen in me starting a new relationship at that time. My child needed me for spiritual, emotional and intellectual support. It was my pleasure to put my needs on the back burner and be there for my son. He meant the world to me and I didn't want him hurt anymore after his real father walked out on us a couple of years earlier when he was only ten. My ex-husband Thomas turned out to be a real asshole. Don't get me wrong. At first we had a loving relationship. He loved me and our son and was always there for us. His family meant the world to him. After awhile though, he became restless and bored in the relationship. He was looking for something else only he didn't know what that something else was. He became distant and soon we stopped talking at all. I just assumed that we were in a marital stump from years of repetitious marital activity and maybe he was a little bored. I had no clue that he wanted to end our marriage. One afternoon I came home early from work because I wasn't feeling well and he was already home from work. I walked into the house, went upstairs to our bedroom and there he was packing his suitcases.

"What are you doing home?" I asked curiously. "Where are you going?"

He looked at me with a blank look on his face and said, "I'm leaving you Michelle. I have to get out of here."

I was shocked. "Get out of here? Get out of where? You want to get out of your own home with your wife and son? What the hell are you talking about? What about me? What about our marriage? What about your son? Are you leaving him too?"

"I will always love our son but, I just don't have it in me to give to him right now. I need time to figure things out."

"Figure things out? Our ten-year-old son needs time to figure things out and he needs both of us to do it. You are a grown fucking man. The only thing you need to figure out is that you have a ten-year-old son who needs you. What's the matter with you? Is there another woman?"

"Michelle there's no other woman."

"Well, is it another man?" I asked.

"No! Don't play me like that. There is no damn man. I'm straight. I'm not confused about that."

"Well, if there is no woman or man what the hell is it? Make me understand what is going on with you. Look, we can sit down and calmly talk about whatever it is that is bothering you. Maybe I can help you. I am your wife and I love you. We can work through anything. Let me help you. Please."

"Look Michelle, I don't want to hurt you but you're not hearing me," he responded with frustration. "I don't want to do this anymore. There's nothing more I can say. I'm out of here. Goodbye Michelle."

My man was acting like a teenager running away from home to find himself in the world. The only problem was that he wasn't a teenager. He was a husband with a wife and a child and he should have found himself years ago. He closed his luggage, picked them up off the bed and walked downstairs. I was crying hysterically as I ran down the stairs after him. "Thomas please don't leave us," I cried out. "I love you. I need you. We need you. What about your son? What about your son? Whatever it is we can work it out. Don't destroy us like this. Please, I'm begging you."

He turned around and looked at me with a blank look on his face. "I'm sorry Michelle. I don't want to hurt you but I have to leave. Kiss Tommy for me and tell him that I love him." He was completely abdicating his responsibilities as a father. He was abandoning his son even though he knew he was the love of our child's life. How could he hurt a sweet innocent young child like this? What kind of soul did he have? How could he sleep at night knowing what he had decided to do to his son? What words did he tell himself to convince him that this type of behavior was acceptable? I couldn't believe that he had emotionally abandoned the both of us like this. Ladies, why is it so easy for a man to just walk out on his children and family without even looking back? Could you ever walk away from your children like that and not even tell them goodbye? What if you were separated from your children and knew that you would never see them again? How would you feel?

"You tell him yourself!" I yelled angrily. "What the hell do you mean by walking out on him like this without even saying goodbye or giving him an explanation? That little boy deserves an explanation from you. He deserves better than this. Be a man and talk to your son."

He looked at me with a blank look on his face and said nothing for a few seconds. "Goodbye Michelle," he said emotionless.

He turned and just walked out like a fucking coward. I watched the love of my life walk out the door and leave me and his only son behind like scraps that he didn't need or want anymore. He showed no signs of remorse or regret. It seemed to me that he was actually relieved that he wasn't responsible for us anymore. Leaving us was actually easy for him. It could never be easy for me to separate myself from my son. In fact, losing my son would kill me inside. My spirit would die. I loved our child just that much. Where was my husband's love? I couldn't understand this. I couldn't understand him. I fell to the floor and cried for over an hour. I couldn't believe that the man I loved, my husband of ten years just walked out the door. I felt so hurt. I was not only hurt for myself but for our son as well. His daddy was his hero. His daddy was the love of his life. He worshipped his daddy. My son was a very sensitive little boy. He loved his daddy so much and would probably blame himself for his dad walking out. How could I hurt this sweet child like this by telling him that his daddy was gone?

I cried out, "Oh God. Please help me."

It was almost time for Tommy to come home from school. The school bus dropped him off at our front door. I had gotten up off the floor and ran to the bathroom just in time to wash the tears from my eyes and freshen up my face before my son saw me. When the school bus arrived I opened the front door of the house and greeted my son. I gave him a big hug and held onto him tightly. My son being a ten year old boy was embarrassed and pulled away from me.

"Ah mom," he said with embarrassment.

I smiled and said, "Come on big man let's go inside."

A couple of school boys on the bus yelled out the window, "Mama's boy! Mama's boy!" They started laughing.

The school bus monitor yelled, "Boys that's enough. Don't yell out the window like that. Sit down."

The bus pulled off. I escorted my son on into the house and all the while he was just chatting away about his day at school. He was so excited as he talked that I was surprised he had time to breathe.

"Mom guess what happened today," he said with excitement.

"What honey?"

"Today Mrs. Caitlin gave us our math tests back and I got it all right. Mom you have to fill out the paper so I can go on the field trip to the aquarium next month. If I don't turn the permission form in on time I won't be able to go. Dad already said I can go. Remember mom? What time is dad coming come? He promised to play ball with me when he came home from work. Can I go outside after I have a snack? Huh mom?"

I laughed and said, "Calm down honey."

He was so excited that I didn't have the heart to tell him at that moment that his daddy had walked out on us. Besides, I hadn't had time to deal with this myself and I still didn't know exactly how I was going to explain all this to my son. I had to put his needs and feelings above my own hurt. I had to be careful and delicate. I couldn't just rush into something like this. I put my son's things away and hung up his coat on the rack. I fixed him a snack as he started on his homework. He knew that he would not be able to go outside to play unless his homework was at least started. I fed him and let him go out to play. While he was outside I called his father Thomas and begged him to come back home.

He answered his cell phone and said, "Hello."

"Thomas it's me Michelle. I want you to know that your son Tommy is home from school and he's already asking for you. Honey, please come home and let's work this out. Tommy needs you. He even remembered that you promised him since last week to come home early from work and play ball with him. Don't hurt him like this. He's just an innocent child. He's just a ten year old baby."

"I don't want to hurt him but I have to do what's right for me," he responded selfishly.

"What do you mean you have to do what's right for you?" I whispered angrily. "You are a selfish bastard! What about doing what's right for your son?"

"Michelle, don't call me with this. You have to deal with our son. I told you I don't want to do this anymore. I'm hanging up now. Don't call me again. You'll be receiving divorce papers from my lawyer soon. Just sign them and let's get this over quickly. I don't want to drag this on. You can have whatever you want. I won't fight you on it. Bye Michelle."

"Thomas! Thomas! Don't you dare hang up on me. Thomas!" He hung up.

When my son came back in from playing I told him to take his bath and put his pajamas on. I didn't tell him that I had just spoken with his father. I didn't want him to know that after I called his daddy he didn't want to even speak to his son. He would never understand. It would break his little heart. My son would somehow internalize that it was all his fault. He would blame himself for the ending of the marriage. I refused to allow that to happen. Ladies, why do men do this to their children especially their sons? How could they just walk away from them and never look back? Sometimes, I just don't understand men at all.

After he cleaned himself up I said, "Come on honey. Dinner is ready."

"What are we having?" he asked.

"We're having spaghetti and meatballs."

"Alright!" he responded with excitement. "I love spaghetti."

"Ok big man. Let's eat. I don't want the dinner to get cold."

After my son finished eating dinner he went to his room to finish his homework.

I came into his room and said, "Tommy honey I have to talk to you."

"What about mom?"

"I have to talk to you about daddy," I said cautiously. I didn't think that it was right for me to tell my son at that moment that his father had walked out on us. I needed more time.

Instead I said, "Tommy your dad is going to be living away from home for a little while."

"Dad is going to be living away from home? What do you mean mom? Where is he going? How long is he gonna be gone? I don't want dad to live away. I want him to stay here with us."

"Tommy I'm not sure exactly how long, but your dad and mom need to be apart for a little while. We still love each other and we will always, always love you. It's just that sometimes grownups need to be apart for a little while to think things out. Remember honey that this is not your fault and your daddy loves you a lot. You didn't do anything wrong. This has nothing to do with you. Ok?" Tommy started to cry and I held onto my son and comforted him.

It had been two years since Thomas walked out on us. Our son was now twelve. Thomas did pay child support and whatever our son needed he provided for financially. That is all. He abandoned our son emotionally. At times he would call and speak to Tommy and make promises that he never kept. He would promise to visit and never show up. He would promise that my son could come and spend some time with him but at the last minute he would call back and cancel the plans. There were missed birthday parties and missed holidays. After awhile my son stopped asking about him. But I could tell that he missed his daddy very much. Then one day out of the blue I received divorce papers from my husband. He offered me generous child support and full custody of Tommy. He didn't even want visitation rights. It was as though he had just thrown us away like garbage. Still to this day I don't know what went wrong. What happened? What did I do wrong? I thought things were good with us. Was I blind? What did I miss? Am I this stupid? And then I thought about all the things I had done over the years to please this man and I realized that it wasn't me. It wasn't me at all. Thomas was just a selfish bastard! Even if he begged me to take him back at this point I never would. After everything he had done to me and the way he hurt our son, I never wanted to see him again. I took the divorce papers to a lawyer and had her look them over. She recommended that I sign the papers after she carefully examined them. She was relieved that my ex-husband was giving me all that my child and I needed and being so generous with the wealth that we had accumulated over the years. He wasn't fighting me on anything financial. He only fought me on the issue of him being a part of his son's life. I wanted him to be there for his son. He refused.

"Michelle I've reviewed the divorce papers that your husband's attorney sent you and I have to say that I am pleased," my lawyer Deborah Spellings said with enthusiasm. "Your husband is practically giving you and your son everything. It appears that he doesn't want anything. He is offering you the house that you currently reside in now, your vacation home in Malibu, California, four-thousand dollars a month in child support, and a lump sum payment of three hundred thousand dollars. That is pretty much everything that the two of you have accumulated in the ten years of your marriage. I think he is being very generous and you should sign the papers as soon as possible."

I did as she recommended. I signed the divorce papers. I was now a single woman again. I no longer had a husband. I was relieved and saddened at the same time. It wasn't as easy as I thought ending my relationship with my husband in the presence of a lawyer. It seemed cold and devastating. Yet it was relieving at the same time.

"Are you alright?" she asked compassionately.

"I'm fine. It's been two years and finally we can get on with our lives. I have to admit, I never thought that my marriage would end like this. I always believed that my marriage would last forever. I thought that my husband and I would grow old together. Well, it's over now. I'm divorced. I'm a cliché now. I'm your typical divorced American woman. They say that one in five marriages end up in divorce. Now I believe it. I am now a statistic. Great."

"I know it's hard," she said sympathetically. "These things are never easy, especially if you have children. But, at least you and your son will be provided for. You'll be alright. Just give yourself some time to get adjusted to being single again. Allow yourself some time to grieve over the ending of your marriage. You and your son will heal in time. If you need anything please call me. I'm more than your lawyer. I'm your friend."

After I had finished signing the papers I turned them over to her. My divorce was finalized. I was now a single mom with a now twelve-year-old child to raise. It was a Monday morning and I had to get ready for work and send Tommy off to school. I yelled up the stairs, "Tommy it's getting late honey. Get up. It's time for school."

Tommy was still in bed. He moaned and then rolled over pulling the covers over his head. He was still half asleep and didn't want to get up yet.

Ladies, some of you know exactly how hard it is to get your children up for school. It's like waking up zombies. I walked into the kitchen to fix breakfast. I made myself a cup of coffee and took a few sips. I reached for a frying pan and placed it on the stove. I grabbed eggs, bread, butter, bacon and jelly from inside the refrigerator and placed them on the counter. I put four pieces of bacon in the frying pan and turned the burner on low so the bacon could cook slowly. I buttered four slices of bread and placed them in the toaster. I realized that Tommy hadn't come down yet so I rushed up the stairs and headed for his bedroom. I knocked on the door and then opened it. I smiled and then walked over to the bed where my son was still sleeping. I pulled the covers off his head and tickled him. He laughed and wiggled as I tickled him.

"Come on honey," I said. "Get up."

Tommy got out of bed and went into the bathroom to get ready for school. I went back downstairs to finish fixing breakfast. After Tommy dressed himself he came downstairs and we ate breakfast together. He watched cartoons as we ate and then turned on the early morning news to see what was being served for lunch at his school. He liked what they were going to serve so I gave him lunch money.

I heard the school bus driver honk the horn and I said, "The school bus is here. Come on honey. Let's go. We're both going to be late." He grabbed his book bag and coat and ran out the door.

"Tommy put your coat on," I yelled as he ran out the door. "It's cold outside."

"Ok mom," he yelled out. He started to put his coat on as he ran to the bus. He got on the school bus and it pulled away. I waved as the school bus pulled off. I didn't even know if Tommy saw me or not. I finished my coffee, got dressed and headed out the door for work.

While at work later that morning one of my co-workers named Donna came up to my area and peeped over the divider. She was sucking on a lollypop as she always did.

"Hey chick! How's it going?" she asked.

"Hi Donna. How was your weekend?"

Donna was a bubbly chick who was always in a good mood. She was outgoing, cheerful and the life of the party. She was a hard worker but she also knew how to play hard and have a good time. She was also a little loud but a lot of fun to be around. I really liked her a lot and enjoyed our ladies nights out together. Occasionally, we would go out to dinner, see a movie together or even go out to a club every once in awhile. It was fun having someone to hang out with even if she was a few years younger than I was at only twenty-four.

"My weekend was hot," she replied. "I went out with this sexy guy. My god he was fine. He took me out to dinner and of course we winded up back at his place where we burned a hole in the floor. We never did make it to the bedroom. He made love to me right there on the floor. Oh my god it was fantastic! It was the best sex that I've had in years. This guy is like a Greek god. His penis should be bronzed. It should be placed in a glass display case surrounded by armed guards in a museum for all women to gaze upon. He had the biggest Johnson I've ever seen. His name is Ricardo. I think he's Italian, French or some shit. Well if he isn't who cares? I'm definitely, definitely going to see him again."

She then said with her sweet I need you to do me a favor voice, "In fact, he gave me a couple of tickets to an art exhibit showing at a gallery that my friend Jacqueline Bijoux owns. I think the artist's name is Damon Douvour or something. Who cares? Anyway, he's supposed to be new, up and coming. He's the next 'it' thing in the art world. I heard he is hot too. I want to see his work. I might buy something. You might even find something you like. Come on. You know you want to go." Donna held two tickets up in the air and flaunted them in my face. "I know you are going to go with me. Please, please Michelle? My new guy Ricardo is going to meet me there and I don't want to show up alone. It's sexy when you show up to an event like this with another hot chick. Guys like that shit. It might get him thinking about a threesome. Say you'll go with me."

"I'll go with you if you shut up and if I can get my sister to baby-sit for me, ok? But, just forget about that threesome shit. It ain't happening."

She laughed and asked, "You're going to have your sister baby-sit? You're so paranoid. Tommy's twelve already. Don't treat him like a baby. He's responsible enough. He's much more mature for his age. He's like a mini man. He can watch himself."

"God help any children that you may have," I said with great concern. "I have now become terrified of ever leaving any child of mine with you. I wouldn't be surprised if you served them liquor and offered them a cigarette and a cup of coffee to unwind. Obviously you are not a mother. If you were you'd know there is no way in hell that I'm going to leave my twelve-year-old son alone in my house. He would destroy it and possibly himself in the process. What's the matter with you?"

She smiled and said, "I'm not that bad. Damn! I would never allow a child to smoke a cigarette or drink liquor. You actually think I would try to destroy the innocence of a child? Besides, there are millions of single moms in the world who have to work hard to make ends meet and their child has to stay at home until they get home from work. Those kids are surviving.

These are trying times and women are doing whatever they have to in order to survive. They're doing the best they can for their families."

"I know this Donna. I'm not knocking any of those women. I have mad respect for all of them. But I will feel much better if my sister watches my son. Humor me, ok? I have to get back to work. I'll get back to you later. Just say good-bye Donna."

"Ok, ok I'm going. I have to get back to work too before I get fired. Get your sister to baby-sit. Let me know at the end of the day if you are going with me or not. Here's your ticket." She reached out and handed me one of the tickets to the art gallery.

I snatched it out of her hand and said, "Say goodbye Donna."

She said sarcastically, "Goodbye Donna." She went back to her desk.

I smiled as she left my office. I picked up the phone to call my sister Ellen. I hesitated for a moment because I really wasn't in the mood to listen to her complaints and bullshit about why she couldn't watch Tommy that night. I had done a lot of favors for her in the past and she owed me. It was time for me to collect.

She answered the phone and I said, "Ellen hi. It's me. It's your sweet sexy gorgeous diva sister. Don't say no before you hear me out. I've done a lot of shit for you in the past. You owe me and I'm collecting now. I need you to watch Tommy tonight. Please?" I pleaded.

"Damn! This is short notice. What if I would have had plans for tonight?"

"Well do you have plans for tonight?"

"No, but what if I did? You are calling me on such short notice."

"It doesn't matter if I'm calling you on short notice now does it? You don't have any plans for tonight, remember?"

She started to ask, "But what if...?"

I interrupted her and said, "Ellen stop being a bitch! Are you going to baby-sit for me or not? I've loaned you money. I've loaned you my car. I've loaned you clothes and jewelry some of which you have never returned. I never complained. Whenever you've needed me I have always been there."

She laughed and said, "Ok you manipulative bitch. Calm down. I'll watch Tommy tonight. I haven't spent time with my only nephew lately anyway. I miss him. It'll be cool. What time do you need me to come over?"

I told her to come over at 7:00 that evening. She finally agreed. At the end of the day Donna came up to me as I was heading out the door.

"So did you find someone to watch Tommy?"

"Yeah I did as a matter of fact. My sister Ellen is going to watch him. I'll meet you in front of the art gallery around 8:30 tonight. Be on time. Don't leave me standing outside looking like a desperate fool who can't get a date. If you don't show up on time I'm going to kill you. Ok?"

"Ok girl. Calm down. I promise. I'll be on time. I'm not going to leave you standing outside looking like a fool. I can't wait to see my new hot sexy Italian stallion tonight. Or is he French? I can't remember. Well, who cares? I'm going to ride that man like a cowgirl in Texas. Oooh! I'm getting turned on just thinking about him. You're going to go crazy when you see him. Thanks for coming with me tonight. I knew I could count on you. Hey, there are going to be a lot of hot single well-educated successful men there tonight. If you play your cards right you could hook up with one. Wear something short and sexy tonight. Don't show up looking like a grandma. Don't be afraid to show cleavage. Let your puppies hang out. Let them dangle so the men can see them."

I said sarcastically, "If you're referring to my breasts then forget it. Donna your puppies hang out enough for the both of us. My puppies are staying in the kennel tonight. I have no interest in hooking up with a dog tonight. Every time I do I end up with fleas. If a dog comes panting at me tonight he is going to get his feelings hurt and his dick chopped off. I swear I'll knee him right in the balls."

Donna smiled and said, "Damn girl. You're such a ball buster. Instead of kneeing balls you need to play with some. Juggle some balls tonight. You know you want to. It's been a long time. You're going to hook up tonight. I can just feel it. You need to let some hot guy peel all the spider webs out of your pussy and go exploring."

I said angrily, "Say goodbye Donna."

She laughed and said, "I'll see you later. Remember, show cleavage. Show cleavage."

Ellen got to the house on time which was unusual for her. My sister was always late for everything. But for some unknown reason she was on time that night. Tommy opened up the door and let her into the house. I was upstairs getting dressed.

Tommy gave Ellen a big hug and said, "Hello Aunt Ellen. Mom says you're going to stay with me tonight. You know I really am old enough to watch myself. I'm not a baby. I'm twelve."

"I know honey. You're almost a man now. Look how tall you're getting. Soon you're going to be taller than me. Wait! What is that I see growing out of your face? Come here." Ellen walked up close to my son. "Is that a mustache growing out of your face? I see a hair. Here let me pluck it." She reached over to my son's face and pulled out a single strand of hair.

My son said sarcastically, "Very funny Aunt Ellen."

She laughed and said, "I'm just teasing you baby. I know you're growing up. But we both know how your mom is. You'll be fifteen and she will still worry about you. She'll probably still be burping you when you're twenty. I brought some junk food full of calories to ruin your appetite and get you fat and of course I brought movies that your mom wouldn't approve of for us to watch. These movies have nothing on them but gore, blood and zombies eating people. You're going to love this stuff. This is our chance to drive your mom crazy. It's gonna be cool. Where's your mom anyway?"

"She's upstairs getting ready to go out to the art show."

"Why don't you go into the living room and start one of these movies. I'll be in to join you soon. I want to go up and talk to your mom for a few minutes first. And don't start the popcorn yet. Wait for me. Ok?"

He said sarcastically, "Ok Auntie."

She laughed and said jokingly, "Smart ass!" She ran up the stairs to the bedroom where I was. As she ran up the stairs she yelled out, "Michelle it's me Ellen. I'm here. I'm coming up." She walked into the bedroom and said, "Hi chick. Where are you going tonight? You look sexy in that cute short red dress and your stiletto high heels. I haven't seen you look this good in a long time. You got a hot date finally? It's been two years Michelle since Thomas walked out on you and Tommy. It's about time you got yourself a new man."

"Oh please Ellen. The last thing I care about is a damn man. After everything that bastard Thomas put me and my son through it's going to be a very long time before I trust another man. All men are dogs. You can't trust any of them. I've had enough for now. I just want to take care of my son and live my life. That's it."

"Don't be like that honey," she said with concern. "There are a lot of good men left in the world. You just need to hook up with the right one. He's out there. He's whispering your name now as we speak. Part of living your life is being in a relationship with someone you love. You have to get on with your life Michelle."

"When did you become so damn intellectual? Ellen look, I don't have time for this right now. I'm going to be late. I have to go. Watch after my baby. Ok?"

"What baby? The boy is twelve. This conversation is not over Michelle. We're going to talk about this some more. You hear me?"

I ignored her and headed down the stairs. I went into the living room and said goodbye to my son who was watching one of the movies that Ellen had brought over.

I tried to kiss my son on the cheek but he said, "Mom, please stop."

I said, "Ok my big man. I'll leave you alone. Mind your Aunt Ellen. Do whatever she says. Is your homework all done?"

"Yes, I did it all."

"Don't stay up too late big man. Remember you have school tomorrow."

I looked at the television and realized that my son was watching gory violence. My sister had brought over a horror film for her and my son to watch. In the movie there were zombies eating people and there were blood and body parts everywhere. It was disgusting. I couldn't believe my sister and my son watched that shit. Ellen jumped on the couch with Tommy and opened up a bag of potato chips.

"Ellen I can't believe you brought this violence over for my son to watch and don't give him too much junk. Ok? And make sure he doesn't stay up all night long. He has school tomorrow."

The two of them looked at each other and giggled. They weren't paying me any attention. I had to realize that my son wasn't a baby anymore and I had to start letting go. I had to lighten up. Next year he was going to be a teenager and a couple years after that he was going to start dating. I still remember when he was a baby and I had to change his diapers. In a few years he would be a man and would go out into the world on his own. I would be alone without my son or my ex-husband. It was a frightening thought. I would literally have to start my life over. I left the house, got in my car and headed to the art gallery to meet up with my friend Donna.

I arrived at the art gallery in Miami at around 8:30 p.m. just as I had said. A lot of people were arriving in their luxury cars and chauffeur driven limousines. There were a lot of successful well dressed professional people at the event that evening. They were all extremely wealthy. I felt a little out of place. I made a good living but I was no where near their league. The men were wearing expensive Italian suits and the women were dressed in their finest designer dresses. They wore diamond jewelry and their hair and make-up was perfect. I waited outside for about five minutes and then Donna showed up.

She ran up the stairs and said, "Sorry I'm late. How long have you been waiting for me?"

"I just got here about five minutes ago," I responded. "I haven't been waiting long. Come on lets go on in."

She said excitedly, "You followed my advice. You let them dangle. You let your puppies out of the kennel. You're such a whore. Good for you. You look hot tonight. That little sexy short red dress you're wearing is hot. You're going to turn heads tonight and I mean that literally. You're going to hook up tonight. Watch and see."

"Come on mini fake sex guru," I responded sarcastically. "Let's go inside."

We headed on inside the art gallery. There were a lot of people at the art exhibit and the artwork was spectacular. Donna's friend Jacqueline Bijoux who owned the art gallery came up to us. She greeted Donna and introduced herself to me. She was a woman of unusual eloquence and impeccable style. She was polished, classy and her taste in art, food, wine and clothes was undeniable. She reminded me of an elegant 1930's French actress. She was a stunning tall French woman who had moved to the states a few years ago to open her own art gallery in Miami, Florida. She had a distinctly French sensuality about her that made her quite sexy. She was an extremely driven woman and that's what led to her success thus far. She was about thirty-five years old. She was very beautiful and dressed impeccably. She wore only the finest designer clothes and very expensive diamond jewelry. She already had a successful gallery in France that was world known. She was a very important lady in the art world and her opinion mattered. When she spoke people listened. Jacqueline told me that the artist was new and upcoming and that one day his work was going to be known world wide. I believed her.

Damon Douvour's paintings were young, exciting and extremely beautiful. His work was eclectic. I really liked his style. He had a lot of talent that needed to be seen by everyone. Damon walked up to us and kissed Jacqueline on the cheek.

She smiled and said, "Damon darling. The show is a success. Look at all the people who showed up tonight. They came to see you and your work. After tonight you are going to be known by everyone who is anybody. I already have orders coming in for your paintings. You did it. Darling you will never lose that certain je ne sais quoi quality about you. You have the 'it' factor and you are very talented. I simply adore you," she said as she pinched his cheeks. "You have a devilish little boy way about you that women simply adore." He laughed in a kind of fake boyish way.

"No. You did it," Damon replied unconvincingly. He was obviously a conceited, cocky asshole. "None of this could be possible if it weren't for you and all the hard work you put into making this gala a success. I will forever be indebted to you."

"Thank you darling," Jacqueline responded. "Let me introduce you to a friend of mine. Her name is Donna."

Damon took Donna's hand and kissed it. I thought he was going to suck the skin right off her hand.

He said in an unconvincingly fake French sexy voice, "It's a pleasure to meet you. You are very beautiful. Do you like my work?"

His fake French accent was pathetic. He was obviously from Brooklyn, New York. You could tell just by listening to him speak. He was very beguiling to women, or so he thought. In actuality, women found him to be rather obnoxious and annoying. He was trying too hard.

Donna blushed and said, "Likewise. I mean I'm honored to meet you too. Your paintings are beautiful. You are very talented."

Jacqueline Bijoux smiled and said, "See. Even she likes your work. I told you that you were a brilliant artist. Now you will believe me."

"And who is this lovely woman standing next to you?" he asked.

Donna introduced me to him. She said, "Oh. This is my best friend Michelle. We work together."

Damon Douvour looked at me like I was a piece of candy and he was going to lick me. The very idea was revolting. I thought that at any second he was going to start drooling. I wasn't turned on sexually by him at all. He reminded me of an oversexed international playboy. He definitely wasn't my type.

"Do you see anything you like?" he asked sarcastically. He was referring to himself. I wanted him to know immediately that I wasn't interested.

"Yes. I see a painting right over there that I might be interested in purchasing." He was a little disappointed that I wasn't referring to him.

Jacqueline smiled and said to him, "Come darling. I have some patrons I want you to meet. They simply adore your work. Come darling." Jacqueline led Damon away from us. I was extremely relieved. The waiters walked around and offered everyone a glass of champagne. Donna and I separated as I walked up to a beautiful painting and gazed at it. The painting was that of an outdoor urban setting. In the painting set in 1930's New York people were out enjoying a beautiful Sunday afternoon. They were dressed in their Sunday's best clothes and were taking a stroll. It was lovely.

A mysterious man walked up to me and asked, "Isn't this piece extraordinary?"

"Yes. It's lovely."

"Do you know the artist?"

"No," I responded. "No I don't. I mean not really. I just met him. His name is Damon Douvour."

The strange man and I looked at each other and smiled at each other knowingly. We both thought Damon was a talented jerk. We both burst out laughing.

"I see you've met him too," I said sarcastically.

He laughed and said, "I'm afraid so."

"I'm here with a friend of mine. Donna. She invited me here tonight. Do you know her?"

"No. I can't say that I do. But, I'm very happy that Donna invited you here tonight. My name is Anthony. It's a pleasure to meet you."

He reached out a hand to me. I reached back and he gently took my hand. We looked into each other's eyes. There was an instant attraction between us. I could tell that he wanted me and I definitely wanted to get to know him better. I hadn't felt like this in a long time. It felt good and right.

By now Donna's man friend Ricardo had arrived and joined her. I glanced at them and my eyes met Donna's. She smiled at me and I could tell that she was definitely infatuated with her new guy. She was right. He was tall, dark and very handsome. I was impressed. I could definitely see why Donna had fallen for him. I was equally interested in the man I had just met. After my vow to not hook up with any man that evening I was surprised and taken aback with myself. I couldn't help myself. I was immediately drawn to him. I couldn't resist him. Anthony was gorgeous and a perfect gentleman. I felt really comfortable with him and was glad that Donna talked me into going to the art exhibit that night. I actually had a really good time. Anthony and I walked around the gallery and enjoyed the beautiful paintings. He got me a glass of champagne and as we walked we enjoyed each other's company and the interesting conversation that we were engaged in. He obviously was well educated and had traveled the world. Anthony had a lot to say and what he said was interesting. We talked about art, religion, archaeology, love, sex and relationships. We had similar tastes and interests. It was amazing how compatible we were. At the end of the evening we exchanged phone numbers and he said he'd give me a call and maybe we could get together again. I agreed.

Donna and her new man Ricardo walked up to us. Donna was clinging onto him for dear life. I thought that any second she was going to swallow him whole. Donna smiled like a school girl with her first love and said, "Well this is him. This is Ricardo. Ricardo I want you to meet a close friend of mine. Her name is Michelle."

He smiled and said, "So you're Michelle. Donna has told me a lot of wonderful things about you. It is a pleasure to finally meet you."

"Donna has told me a lot of wonderful things about you as well Ricardo. I'm happy to meet you also." We shook hands gently.

"We have to go," Donna said. "The evening is not over for us. Ricardo is taking me back to my place. I don't think I'm going to make it to work tomorrow. I'll probably be staying in bed most of the day."

"You're a very naughty girl Donna. Don't do anything I wouldn't do."

Donna looked over at Anthony and smiled. She said, "You don't need to follow your own advice Michelle. You need to do everything tonight. Have some fun. Be naughty for once. Remember, you need to get rid of the spider webs," she whispered. Thank goodness neither Ricardo nor Anthony knew what the hell she was talking about. It would have been too embarrassing. Neither one of them needed to know that I hadn't been laid in awhile.

She said to Anthony, "Hello."

He smiled and said, "Hi."

I said goodbye to Donna and Ricardo. They walked off and left the gala. As they were leaving she whispered to me, "He's cute."

Anthony laughed and said, "Wow."

"I know," I responded sarcastically. "She's something else."

Anthony walked me outside and to my car.

Once at my car Anthony asked, "Well are you going to follow your friend's advice?"

"What advice?"

"She told you to be naughty tonight and have a good time," he said sarcastically. "Well?"

"No. I'm not going to be naughty tonight. I'm going home to my son. I have a twelve year old."

He smiled and said, "I see. Well, it was definitely a pleasure meeting you and I'd love to see you again. I had a really good time tonight. Would it be inappropriate for me to kiss you?"

I didn't know this man that well so there was absolutely no way I was going to let him kiss me on the mouth and he knew it. I gave him my hand and he pecked it with his lips. I said good night, got in my car and headed for home. I arrived at home around 1:30 am. Ellen was stretched out on the couch. She was watching television and eating popcorn. Tommy was already sleeping in his room.

"Hey. How was your evening?" she asked.

"It was good. I had a lot of fun. I'm actually glad I decided to go out tonight."

"You look like you had a good time," she said with suspicion. "Damn girl. You're glowing. Tell me all about it. Did you meet any fine men tonight or what?"

"As a matter of fact, I did."

She jumped up off of the couch. Popcorn spilled everywhere. She almost tripped and fell on her ass.

"What!" she yelled out with excitement. "You met someone? Who is he? What does he look like? Is he fine? Is he rich? What kind of car does he drive? Where does he live? Is he married? Tell me everything bitch."

"Calm down Ellen. You're going to wake Tommy. I'll tell you all about it. Just let me get out of these heels. My feet are killing me."

"Well hurry up. I want to hear this."

I slipped my stiletto heels off and plopped down on the couch.

Ellen sat back down and said, "Ooh child! Let me get comfortable so I can hear all the nasty sexy dirty little details. Don't leave anything out. I want to hear it all."

"Well, I did meet a man at the art exhibit. His name is Anthony. He's very handsome and a perfect gentleman. He treated me like a lady. We spent the entire evening together enjoying the artwork and talking about everything, anything. It was wonderful! I haven't felt like this in a long time."

"Forget all that sweet shit." she said impatiently. "Did you fuck him?"

"No Ellen. I didn't. Man I swear. Don't talk like that here. Take it in the street with your friends. I have a child here. Besides, I don't even really know the man. I just met him tonight. Damn you're such a whore."

"You didn't even let him get to first base? You didn't even let him touch your puppies?"

I said angrily, "No Ellen. If you're referring to my breasts, then no. He didn't touch anything. Why do you and Donna keep calling my breasts puppies? You two are sick."

She laughed and said, "Well it's been two years since you had some and I know you must be horny by now. If he's that fine go for it. Do him. I would."

"I know you would. We all know you would. You'd do a psychopath just to get laid. Like I said, I don't really know the man and I would like to take my time and get to know him. For all I know he could be a damn serial killer or something. You also forget that I have a son who is your nephew. I have to be careful what man I bring home. My son has been hurt enough. I have to protect him."

"You're right. I care about my nephew too. I get it. I get it. Well I'm tired," she said. "I'm going home."

"Ellen it's late," I said with concern. "Why don't you just stay here tonight? You don't want to be driving home this time of morning. It's dangerous out there. If you leave here now I'll just worry about you all night. You know me."

"No," Ellen said defiantly. "I'm not staying here tonight. I want to go home. I tell you what, I'll call and let you know as soon as I get home that I'm Ok. How about that mother?"

"I know that I'm not your mother. I am however your sister and I worry about you. That is all. Drive safe and call me like you promised. Don't make me worry about you," I said with reservation. "Ellen, don't get home and forget to call me. I know you. You'll get home, jump into bed and forget all about me. If you do I swear you won't have to worry about the sick asses out there. I will personally kill you myself."

"I swear I'll call mommy, she said sarcastically. Don't worry." She left the house and headed for home. I started to get ready for bed. I still had to get up early and go to work. After about a half an hour the phone rang. It was Ellen. She had made it home safely and was checking in with me. I said good night to her. "Goodnight mommy," she said sarcastically and then she hung up.

The next morning I was exhausted and almost over slept, but I had to go to work. I got Tommy up quickly and got him ready for school. I only had time to give him a bowl of cereal for breakfast and give myself a cup of coffee and a danish. As soon as we started eating the school bus arrived and the bus driver honked his horn. Tommy took a few more spoonfuls of cereal and put the entire bowl up to his mouth and drank the milk.

"Let's go Tommy. The bus is here."

"Ok mom."

He put the bowl down, grabbed his book bag and ran out the door to the bus. I finished my coffee and went on in to work. I was at my desk when Donna came over and leaned over the divider. As usual she was sucking on a lollypop.

She yelled, "You slut. Who was that handsome man you were with last night? His name is Anthony, right? I saw the way you two looked at each other. You two looked like you wanted to jump each other's bones. I could tell you have the hots for him. Did you let him clean the spider webs out of your pussy? You were practically drooling over him."

"I was not drooling over him Donna. Don't talk stupid. No. He didn't go anywhere near my pussy. He was just some guy I met. We talked. That's it."

"Are you going to see him again?" she asked inquisitively. She was obviously trying to get all up into my business.

"I don't know. I'm thinking about it. We'll see. Anyway, I gave him my number and he said he'd call. Let's just wait and see what happens. By the way, I like your new man. You're right. He is fine. The two of you look happy together. Congratulations. I'm glad you found somebody. You deserve to have a good man in your life."

"It looks like we both found somebody," she said happily. "Are you planning on sleeping with him? You know it's been a long time since you've been with a man. Do you even remember how to have sex?"

"Say goodbye Donna."

She laughed and said, "Goodbye, Donna."

She went back to her desk. Anthony called me three days later and invited me out to dinner that Saturday night. I accepted his invitation and had Ellen watch Tommy again. I thought it was a little too soon for Anthony to meet my son because like I said; I didn't really know the man that well. I met Anthony at the restaurant and we had a lovely evening. He was very sweet and gentle and was an excellent conversationalist. I really enjoyed being with him and he made me feel safe. As time went on and we dated more and more I began to trust him. We dated on and off for several weeks before I finally introduced him to my son. They hit it off from the beginning. They became buddies. Anthony took Tommy out everywhere. They went fishing, hiking, boating and Anthony even played ball with him whenever he was able. I was finally happy again. I didn't realize it, but things began to change right after Anthony moved in with us. It was a subtle change at first and then the change was drastic. Tommy couldn't have been happier that Anthony moved in with us. He finally had the father figure that he was longing for. I loved the relationship between the two of them and the way that they interacted with each other. It was as though they fit together. A stranger looking in would swear that Anthony was his natural father.

A few weeks after Anthony moved in and his attitude changed a little he started making small complaints which I didn't take too seriously at the time. I just thought it was three people living together for the first time trying to get adjusted to each other's ways. Then he began to drink a little, especially on the weekends. Again, I wasn't concerned. "What's wrong with a man having a few drinks after work and on the weekends to unwind?" I thought.

Then, Anthony's complaints became more annoying. He started complaining that his shirts weren't ironed well enough or that the eggs weren't cooked the way he liked them. Then he started complaining that the house wasn't clean enough or that his dinner wasn't prepared right. I tried to please him by accommodating his wishes but the complaints kept coming. As he drank more and more he stopped spending so much time with Tommy and this affected my son. Tommy again thought it was something that he had done wrong. He began to believe that there was something wrong with him. The men in his life just kept disappointing him over and over again. I spent more time with Tommy myself and tried to comfort him but it didn't help. Another man had disappointed him and he began to change. The sweet boy I raised started rebelling and getting into trouble at school. He was getting detention every other month for doing things like skipping school, not doing his homework, talking back to teachers, fighting with other students and more. I didn't know what to do. I didn't know how to reach him. I knew that it was my fault for introducing Anthony into his life, but I loved Anthony. I felt torn between the two of them. Ladies, if you had to choose between your man and your child, what would you do? There were other changes with Anthony too. He would spend more and more time away from the house. At first he would get home from work around 6:30pm. Then it was 11:00pm before I saw him each evening. Then on the weekends he didn't come home until 3:00am. I asked him where he was and I got the same weak-ass excuse that most men give women.

"I was working late", he said unconvincingly.

Anthony worked the day shift. How the hell did he suddenly start working past 11.00 pm? It didn't make sense. He was obviously lying to me. We know our men's schedules and what job they have. Ladies listen up. If your man tells you over and over that he had to work late there is a good chance he's lying to you. 99.99% of the time that's just bullshit. Is your man's job even open at that time or has everyone in the company already gone home? Use common sense. Ladies, check your man and find out exactly what the hell he's up to if he's staying out late at night. If he doesn't work the evening shift then most likely he is not working late. I'm sure there are thousands of you out there who have heard that same bullshit excuse before.

Anthony also began to isolate me from my friends and family. It was as though he didn't want anyone to know what an abusive asshole he was. He was also very insecure and didn't want anyone influencing me to leave him. It was all about control. It was about control over me, my son and our lives. In fact, he wanted control over all of his women. He said that my girlfriends were a negative influence on me and that I needed to 'cut them loose' as Anthony would say. When I refused, he started pushing them away one by one himself. I remember one particular moment when a close friend of mine named Rebecca came over to visit on a Saturday afternoon. We had plans to go shopping together. It was hot so we both wore shorts and tee shirts. We wanted to keep cool and believe me when I say that we didn't give a damn about trying to meet men.

"Where the hell are you going dressed like that Michelle?" Anthony yelled as he came out of the garage.

We were both stunned. I couldn't believe that Anthony was embarrassing and disrespecting me like this.

"Anthony, why are you yelling at me like that? What's the matter with you? Dressed like what? I have on shorts and a shirt."

Anthony yelled out in front of my friend, "Dressed like a slut. Like a whore. Don't even think of trying to convince me that you are dressed like that to go shopping. Only women looking to have men stare at their asses would dress in shorts that show their asses like that. I'm not a fucking fool! I know what you two bitches are up to."

My friend was very offended. "Oh hell no!" she said angrily. "He is not my man so I don't have to put up with this. Nobody talks to me like that. I don't know who the hell you think you are. I'm out of here. Good-bye Michelle." She walked away from us and headed for home. I tried to stop her but she wouldn't even listen to me. Anthony apologized to me later, but he had accomplished what he set out to do. He had offended and frightened my friend Rebecca so much she never came back to my house again. She wouldn't even accept my phone calls so that I could apologize to her. His plan to alienate me from my friends was working. I still wanted my friends to come over from time to time and enjoy a quiet evening with us at home. I loved to entertain friends and I thought that if Anthony spent more time with them maybe he would grow to like and respect them. That was a big mistake on my part and it cost me more close friends.

Anthony also decided to get rid of my friend Donna. At first he liked her. When they first met at the art gallery that night he thought that she was very funny. His first response to her was, 'Wow!' Then he became insecure and jealous of our relationship. He began to find her humor annoying. Also, he didn't want her to figure out how controlling and nasty he was with me and my son. He wanted his emotional abuse to remain a secret. Donna was becoming suspicious of his attitude and behavior. She noticed how controlling and disrespectful he was with me. She didn't like it. She grew concerned for me. She decided to try and intervene. She was in my office one day and decided to express her concerns.

"Michelle you know I love you and am only concerned for you. I'm not trying to get in your business but you've changed. I don't like what is happening to you. You used to be so strong and confident. Now you've become nervous and edgy all the time. You're not happy honey. I can see it. Everyone can see it. You forget that I know you. I've known you for a long time honey. You're like a sister to me. I can see something is wrong. We all can see it around here. If Anthony is hurting you or Tommy you need to leave him. Leave him now before it's too late."

Right at that moment Anthony showed up at my office to take me to lunch. He heard the entire conversation and he was furious. He developed a hatred for Donna and at that moment if he knew he could get away with it he would have killed her. He walked into the office and we both turned and looked at him.

I asked uneasily, "Honey what are you doing here? I wasn't expecting you."

"I came to take you out for lunch. Is that ok? Can't we even have lunch together anymore?"

"Of course we can. I just wasn't expecting you. That's all. You remember my friend Donna."

"Yes I remember. Hello Donna."

He gave her such an evil expression that she became frightened.

She smiled uneasily and said, "Anthony. I was just leaving. I have to go. We'll talk later Michelle. Bye."

Donna was scared to even walk past him. She squeezed her way past him and left the office. He wouldn't even move out of the way for her. He just stood his ground defiantly with his arms folded and rolled his eyes at her as she passed him. It was his way of showing her that as a mere woman she was beneath him. She could sense the anger in him.

After she left he said angrily, "I don't like that bitch! What right does she have to get in our business? Who the fuck does she think she is?"

"Anthony she wasn't in our business. She is just concerned for me and Tommy. That's all. She is a good friend and I want to keep her in my life. You don't get to pick and choose which friends I'm allowed to keep in my life. I'm a grown woman. I make my own decisions. I'm not getting rid of Donna and I won't let you either."

Anthony said angrily, "I heard her discussing me when I walked up. Do I look stupid to you? She was telling you to leave me before it was too late. She wants you to leave me before it is too late? What does she think I am going to do to you and Tommy? What the hell does she know? Have you been discussing our business at work? I'm not your enemy Michelle. You know I love you. There is nothing for her to be concerned with. I'm your man and I'll take care of you and Tommy. Ok? Let's get out of here."

He yelled out angrily, "Come on. Let's go!"

"Ok. Ok. I'm coming. Calm down. Damn."

Weeks passed and Anthony became more and more angry that Donna was still a part of my life. Anthony's way of getting rid of Donna was to terrorize her. He put on a black outfit and a black burglar's cap to hide his face and he went to her apartment one evening when I was away with Tommy. She was alone in her apartment and had decided to take a shower. Anthony broke into her apartment as she was in the shower. He was wearing black gloves so his fingerprints wouldn't be traced anywhere in her apartment. He broke the back door window, reached his hand onto the inside doorknob and turned it until it opened. Glass splattered everywhere. Donna didn't hear anything in the shower. She had no idea that a man was in her home unwelcomed. She had no idea of the danger that she was in and that she could be beaten, raped, killed or all of the above. Anthony had his cap pulled over his face so that only his eyes, mouth and lips could be seen. He snuck up the stairs quietly so that Donna couldn't hear him. When he got upstairs he snuck into her bathroom and snatched the shower curtains back. Donna screamed in total terror at the strange man that was standing in front of her naked body. Anthony grabbed her and pulled her out of the bathroom. He dragged her naked wet body out of the bathroom and threw her on the bed. She tried to fight him off but he was too powerful. He climbed on top of her and thrust his pelvis into her. He grouped her bare breasts and tried to kiss her in the mouth. She could smell the alcohol on his breath. She became nauseous. He put his hands between her legs and rubbed her vagina and then he penetrated her with his finger. She started to cry. She knew at that moment he was going to rape her. Anthony wasn't interested in having sex with her. He wanted to take away her self-esteem and her self-worth. He wanted to take away her dignity. He just wanted to humiliate and degrade her. It worked. Even though he didn't penetrate her with his penis she felt as though he had. Anthony didn't want to violate her completely. He just wanted to put her in her place. He wanted to put this mere woman in her place. It was all about power. It was about his power over her. It was about his physical power over any woman. It was about his desire to control all women in his world. He had taken away her sense of safety. Suddenly, he just got up, ran down the stairs and rushed out the door. He disappeared into the night.

Donna was too traumatized to move. She covered herself up with her blanket and cried hysterically. After she felt that he was gone she ran downstairs to see how he had gotten into her apartment. She ran to the back door, closed it and locked it. There was still glass splattered on the floor. She cut her foot on some of the glass and her right foot began to bleed. She screamed out in pain as the glass pierced her flesh. She pulled the glass out of her foot and wrapped it up with a dish towel. She grabbed a butcher's knife out of the kitchen and ran up the stairs to get dressed. After she got dressed she lowered herself on the floor in the corner of her bedroom. She waited to see if the strange man would show up again so she could kill him with the knife. He never came back. She finally got up off of the floor and went into her bathroom. She stepped into the shower with her clothes on. She turned the water on as hot as she could tolerate it. It didn't matter to her if her clothes got wet. She just wanted to wash his touch and smell off of her. She felt that the hot water would somehow make the horrible feeling of him touching her disappear. It didn't work. She lowered herself onto the shower floor with the water pouring down on top of her. She cried hysterically. Donna never did find out that it was Anthony who had terrorized her. She lost self-confidence in herself. She felt totally helpless in the world. She no longer knew how to protect herself in this world of danger and criminals and rapists. She didn't even know if the strange man would come back and finish what he had started. She didn't feel safe in her own home anymore. She became a nervous wreck. When any of us at work tried to speak to her she would just burst out into tears.

I went to her on more than one occasion and asked, "Donna please tell me what is wrong with you. Are you sick? Has your new man Ricardo hurt you? What is going on with you? I'm really worried about you honey. Don't you know that you can trust me and tell me anything? What has happened? Do you need to tell me something? Are you sick?"

Donna would just say, "No honey. I'm not sick. Ricardo is out of the country on business. He'll be back in a few weeks. He hasn't hurt me. I'm not sick and nothing is wrong. I swear. Just leave it alone. Alright?"

There was nothing I could do. If Donna didn't want to confide in me than I couldn't force it out of her. One day she decided that she just couldn't take it anymore. She was literally falling apart. She called her mother and told her that she wanted to leave Miami and return to Houston, Texas. Her mother told her to come home and that she could stay with her parents as long as she wanted to. Donna left her apartment and moved back to Texas with her parents. She never did even say goodbye to us or explain why she was leaving. If Donna would have confessed to me what had happened and called the police to press charges, maybe my son and I wouldn't have been terrorized by Anthony the way we were about to. The police might have figured out that it was Anthony and arrested him. I never saw her again. Anthony accomplished what he wanted. He had gotten rid of Donna.

It was Christmas and I decided to have two couples, Dan & Jessica and Richard & Janet over for a Christmas dinner. Tommy was at my sister's house for the evening. Christmas was all in the air. Everyone in the neighborhood had their houses decorated with beautiful Christmas lights. Everyone was cooking Christmas dinner and you could smell the aroma of delicious food throughout the entire neighborhood. You could see decorated Christmas trees through all the windows with wrapped presents underneath them all. Our house was also beautifully decorated both inside and out. We had a very large pine Christmas tree with an angel on top. There was presents and wrapping paper everywhere. I had hired a Christmas decorating team to come out and put up the outside lights for us. It was spectacular. I was dressed in a sexy black dress. My hair and makeup was perfect.

I stood in front of the full length mirror in our bedroom and said out loud to myself, "Not bad girl. Not bad at all." Anthony was already dressed in a black suit and had already had a couple of drinks. He came into the bedroom where I was and stared at me as he took another sip of his drink.

"You know what? You really should wear your other dress Michelle. You know. Wear the red one that I like."

"Anthony I'm already dressed. The guests will be here soon and besides I feel like wearing this dress tonight. Ok?"

Anthony didn't say anything. He just stared at me for a moment. He then walked over to my closet, took the red dress down and threw it on the bed. "I'll see you downstairs when you take that damn dress off and put this one on," he said angrily. "Hurry up Michelle. The guests will be here soon." He gave me a look that I'll never forget. He looked at me as if he could kill me right then. I can't really explain it. It was a look of pure evil. I was frightened of him. As he walked out of the room he continued to take sips of his drink. To please him and ensure a pleasant evening for everyone I did as he had asked. I reluctantly took my dress off and put the one he wanted me to on. Ladies, wouldn't you do the same thing if you were me?

As I headed downstairs wearing the red dress that he ordered me to put on, the doorbell rang. The two couples arrived at almost the same time. I tried to get Anthony to come with me to greet them at the door but he refused. He was being his stubborn old self and the drinking didn't help any.

"Anthony please come with me to greet our guests," I pleaded. "It wouldn't look good if I went alone. They're our guests."

Anthony yelled out, "To hell with them. They're not my guests. They're your fucking guests. You go greet them. Shit!" He continued to drink.

As I walked to the front door I pleaded with Anthony. "Please behave tonight. Don't ruin this evening for me. Please. I'm begging you."

"Ah, to hell with this," he slurred in a drunken stupor. He continued to drink and get drunk. I opened the front door and both couples were there.

"Hi guys," I said nervously. I was worried about Anthony's behavior. "Come on in." The ladies came in first. We greeted and hugged each other. The men followed.

"Honey here's some dessert that I made for after dinner," Jessica said with pride even though I didn't know why she was so proud. I hated her desert. She was a lousy cook.

"Oh honey. You didn't have to do that. Really. You shouldn't have."

"Oh don't be silly. It was my pleasure," she responded. She handed me the fruit cake that she had made. I absolutely hated fruit cake. Fruit cake at Christmas. It's such a cliché. That should have been a sign to me that the entire evening was going to be totally fucked up. Then my friend Janet greeted and hugged me.

"Thank you for inviting us. We brought the booze," she said with excitement. She was always a little high strung but I really liked her. She was a lot of fun and knew how to turn a boring house party into a lot of fun. "Here are a couple of bottles of wine." She handed me a gift bag with two bottles of wine in it. I had fruit cake in one hand and wine in the other.

Dan and Richard greeted me next. "Hello Michelle," Dan said as he kissed me on the cheek.

"Thanks for inviting me and Janet over to your home Michelle. We don't see you as much as we use to since you hooked up with your new man. I can't wait to meet him. He must be something else for you to abandon us like this.

I want to see who has been keeping you away from us all this time," Richard said sarcastically. They all laughed.

"Well you'll get your chance to meet my man right now. Thank you for the wine Janet. We're gonna drink this tonight. Let me put it on ice to chill. But first let me introduce you to Anthony. He's in the living room. Come on in guys." They followed me into the living room. "Anthony our guests have arrived. This is Jessica & Dan and Richard & Janet."

Everyone said "Hello" to him.

"Can I fix you a drink?" he asked. "What's your poison?"

Dan and Richard had whiskey straight. Jessica had a glass of white wine. I excused myself and took the two bottles of wine that I had in my hand and put them on ice. I placed the fruit cake on the dining room table. Anthony asked Richard's wife Janet what she wanted to drink.

"Nothing," Janet responded. "Thank you. I'm not drinking tonight."

"Nonsense," he said. "If we're all drinking than you're drinking. What'll you have? I got it. You look like a wine person. Let me fix you a glass of wine like Jessica over there."

"No, thank you," Janet responded uneasily. "I don't want any wine tonight, but the rest of you can go ahead and enjoy yourselves."

"Your friend here is irritating the hell out of me Michelle. I say if I must drink then we all must drink." He poured Janet a glass of wine and tried to hand it to her.

Her husband Richard said, "My wife is not drinking tonight Anthony. Let her be. Let that be the end of it."

Anthony gave up. "Ok! Ok! I'll leave her alone. I was just kidding. I was just kidding man. Don't get mad."

He was already a little drunk but he made himself another drink. Everyone was starting to feel a little uneasy at that point. I was upset but I was trying to hide my true feelings from everyone. Anthony was embarrassing me in front of my friends again. I'm sure they could all see the embarrassment on my face.

"Come on everybody," I said. "Let's go eat. Dinner is ready."

I did what a lot of women do. I pretended like nothing was wrong and that Anthony was just having a little fun. I brushed his behavior off as though it was no big deal. I was also hoping that the food would sober him up a little and he would stop embarrassing me. My friends saw right through me and him and were not impressed at all. It was humiliating. We got up and walked to the dining room for dinner. The caterers came in and fixed our plates. We had dinner rolls, salad, glazed ham, macaroni and cheese, string beans and for dessert apple pie a-la-mode and of course the damn fruit cake. Dinner was going great. The food was delicious. We were all engaged in conversation and Anthony was actually behaving himself for a change. The food must have sobered him up a bit as I had hoped. My mind was starting to ease. Then, it happened. My friend Jessica asked something that destroyed the entire evening.

"Hey Michelle, when was the last time that you saw Rebecca?" she asked. "You know I haven't heard from her in awhile. How's she doing?"

Anthony became furious. He remembered that Rebecca was the one who cursed him out when he told us that we dressed like whores in our shorts. He hated her and never wanted me to see her again. He banged his fist on the table. Everyone was startled and stopped eating. We all looked at him in total amazement. "Isn't that the bitch that had you dressing like a prostitute that time Michelle?" He turned to Jessica and yelled out, "I can't believe you have the nerve to mention that whore's name in my house. She's a slut! She's a stupid bitch! Who the hell do you think you are? Do you think you run this shit? Do you think that you can come into me and Michelle's house and disrespect me like this?"

Dan, Jessica's husband, stood up. "Who the hell do you think you're talking to like that?" he asked. "You don't talk to my wife like that. I don't give a damn whose man you are. I will straight up whip your ass if you ever talk to my woman like that again."

"You son-of-a-bitch!" Anthony yelled. "This is my got damned house. I'll say whatever I want to and to whomever I want. And you ain't whipping nobody's ass. You're a stupid weak ass bastard." Anthony was standing at this time and at that moment I knew they were going to start fighting. They were like two gorillas about to pounce on each other. You could sense the testosterone flinging all over the room. I walked over to Anthony and put my hands on his chest.

"Please Anthony," I pleaded. "I'm begging you. Don't do this. These are my friends."

"They used to be your friends. As of right now you don't have any friends. The only friend you need is me. I'm your friend. I'm all you need." He yelled out loud, "Yeah she's my bitch and whoever doesn't like it can kiss my ass!"

All my guests were ready to get the hell out of my house and go home. The men were concerned for their wives. My lady friends were worried about me. None of them wanted to leave me alone with him. They were concerned about him becoming physically violent with me. The evening was obviously over.

"Michelle, are you sure it's ok to leave you here alone with him like this?" Janet asked. "You could always come home with us."

"Oh yes honey. I'm ok. We'll be ok. I'm sorry guys for all of this. I'm sorry the evening was ruined. Anthony just had a little too much to drink.

You guys know how it is. It's the holidays and he is celebrating. You know? He's usually not like this. This is not him. Maybe we can all get together some other time." I knew even when I said it that there was no way in hell that any of these people would ever step foot in my house again. My four guests just looked at each other uneasily and then they quickly left my house. As they hurried out the door they all said good-bye to me and then left. They didn't even bother to speak to Anthony.

Anthony apologized to me for the embarrassment that he caused me again in front of my friends, but he had accomplished what he wanted to. He had alienated me from the rest of my friends. Ladies, have any of you been in a relationship with a man who alienated you from your families and friends so that he could take total control over you? The only ones left were my son, my sister Ellen and my mom. My sister and my mother's first impression of him was that he was an asshole. They never liked him nor did they trust him. They immediately had a gut instinct that something was wrong. I realize now that I should have listened to their instincts. Ladies, have any of you ever had family or friends tell you that you should leave your abusive or controlling man before it was too late? Did you listen to them or just stayed out of fear or love for your man? Unfortunately, my family and friends were right. My mother came over one afternoon to have lunch with me. My son was visiting with friends and Anthony had gone out to run errands. My mother looked at me and couldn't help but see how unhappy I was. Momma always knows these things. They have a six sense about when their baby girls are in trouble. Ladies I'm sure that most of you have that same six sense when it comes to your own daughters. When you were growing up did your mother have that ability? Could she tell that something was wrong in your life or relationships even before you said anything?

"I know what is going on," my mom said with suspicion. "I've heard the stories and rumors. I'm no fool honey. I've been on this earth of ours a very long time and I know more than you think I do. Sweetheart don't you understand. Before I met your father I was right where you are now. I was you. Through all the slaps, punches, choking, verbal abuse and the cheating I told myself it was my fault. I told myself if I could only do better he wouldn't get so angry. I told myself over and over that he really loved me and that he was under a lot of stress. Honey I was just lying to myself the way you are lying to yourself right now. It's not going to get better baby. It's going to spiral out of control until you and that precious grandson of mine are both killed by him." She whispered to me softly, "Leave him. Leave him before it's too late."

My mother was right in that she had been where I was. She grew up in Miami, Florida. She left home one day and moved to New York City to find herself and discover what she wanted to do with her life. That's where she met Philip. My mother was in her late twenties and Philip was about thirty-four years old. He was very handsome and a real ladies man. Women adored him and he used that to his advantage every chance he got. He was never faithful to my mother and when she finally dug up the courage to confront his indiscretions their relationship changed for the worst. He became physically and verbally abusive to her. There were times when he slapped her across the face and times when he would grab her around her neck and push her against the wall. She became more and more terrified of him. She was even afraid to go to sleep at night out of fear of what he might do to her. One evening he came home very late from work. My mother knew that he had been with another woman. She was tired of feeling hurt and humiliated. She was tired of being disrespected by him. She had enough. She confronted him.

"Where have you been?" she asked. "You got off of work hours ago. Dinner is ruined. Why didn't you call me?"

He became furious. He stormed up to her and stood inches away from her face. He stared right into her eyes with a look of rage. She was so frightened that she thought her knees would buckle and she would fall to the floor. He grabbed her around her neck and started to choke her.

"Who do you think you are questioning me like I'm a damn child?" he yelled. "You're going to interrogate me like a criminal? I'm a man and I'll damn well do as I please. Don't you ever speak to me like that again. If you even think of talking to me like that again I swear I'll kill you with my bare hands."

My mother was gasping for air and trying to fight him off of her. It was of no use. He was just too strong for her. Her life flashed in her mind and she thought that evening she was going to die. She closed her eyes and started to pray to God to forgive her for her sins and trespasses. She prayed that God would grant her eternal salvation through the blood that Jesus Christ shed for us all. Then she prayed for the salvation for the man that was about to kill her. She prayed that God would forgive him as well. Suddenly, Philip let her go. He punched a hole in the wall with his fist just inches from her head. He cracked his knuckles and they began to bleed. He was filled with such rage and fury that he felt no pain. He looked at her angrily as though he could have killed her and then he stormed into the bedroom. He slammed the bedroom door so hard after he entered it that my mother thought for sure it would fall right off its hinges. My mother was coughing and gagging. It was hard for her to catch her breath. She fell to the floor and cried hysterically.

My mother was too afraid to move. She slept on the floor that night exactly where she had fallen. The next morning they went through what is referred to by mental health experts as the "Honeymoon Phase." He pretended as though the previous evening had never happened. Philip got up, showered and got dressed.

He walked over to my mother and whispered softly, "Come on baby. Get up. It's ok now. I'm not mad anymore. Come on now." He helped her up off of the floor. He said, "Now, you see what happens when you piss me off? Come on. Don't be mad. Give me a kiss." He kissed her on the mouth. As he did she became nauseas and was totally repulsed by his touch. When he finished he said, "Now be a good girl and fix me some breakfast. I'm hungry. Fix yourself something too. You must be starved."

My mother did as he asked out of fear of being beaten again. As she was cooking she hid her face so he couldn't see her tears. After months of his abuse she had enough. One day she waited for him to leave for work. After he was gone she ran through the apartment and gathered her things and put them into a suitcase. She moved as quickly as she could. She was terrified that he would come back and catch her trying to leave. She caught a cab to the train station and took a train back to Florida to be with her family. She never saw Philip again. Thank goodness she had never married him nor had any children with him. She was able to cut all ties to him.

As my mother grew stronger and stronger emotionally and spiritually her fears about men subsided. She was able to love again without fear of getting physically or emotionally abused. My father was the most affectionate man that she had ever met. A couple years later she met and fell in love with him and he turned out to be the love of her life. When he was murdered we weren't sure that my mother would survive without him. But she survived and was stronger than ever. I admired her strength. My father's death was hard on my mom. He was a good man, a good husband and a good father. He was the best. He spent his entire marriage trying to make us happy and giving us everything we wanted and needed. He had decided early on in the marriage between him and my mother to devote his life trying to make us happy. He was the one true love of my mom's life and he treated her with respect and dignity. He treated her like a queen and then one day he was gone. My mother had never been successful with men in her younger years but my father changed that. I wasn't very successful with men either. I guess like mother like daughter.

My father Jonathan Weber worked at a prestigious law firm in Miami. He had no idea of the danger that he was in. He was a business attorney who had hopes of one day becoming a full partner in his firm. What he didn't know was that his law firm had heavy ties to the mob. They were heavy into money laundering and more criminal activities. One day my father accidentally stumbled across some incriminating documents that he should never have seen. They were financial records of bills to known criminals in the underworld. He realized that his associates were actually taking money from men who had been in the media as being involved with the Mafia. My father realized that not only was his life in danger but his wife and two daughters were also. His law associates were colluding with known felons. My father decided to conduct his own undercover investigation to dig up more information. He had decided to search for more information and evidence and turn it over to the federal government. He decided to become a whistle blower, a traitor to his own firm and risk being disbarred. The future of the firm rested in his hands. He had the power and that didn't sit well with the partners in his firm. He had to be killed. Their ruthlessness resulted in the death of my father.

Over several weeks my father secretly searched records, files and computer software of several of his associates in the law firm. He found a lot of incriminating evidence that could potentially put his law associates in prison for years. He also found out that they had illegally stashed millions of dollars in cash in offshore banks in the Cayman Islands and had not paid taxes on any of it. It was then that he decided to turn his associates over to the federal government for tax evasion rather than disclose confidential client and attorney information. This would put his associates in prison for years without getting my father disbarred. He had figured out a way to stop them without destroying his own life and career. What my father's associates didn't know was that he was quite the computer hacker that they should fear. He could get into almost any computer file. He made copies of records and of information off of disks that proved that they had been cheating on their tax returns for years. What he didn't know was that the partners in the firm had become suspicious. They knew that someone within the firm was stealing secret information and all evidence pointed to my father. They immediately took steps to ensure that their private files could never be breeched again. They hired a top security team to come into the firm and change all the locks and codes to high tech security systems. There were four partners in the law firm and they were all aware of the criminal activities going on. They were all in on it. They called a private meeting one evening after my father and the other associates had left the building for home. Tom Berenger, William Stanford, Harry Henderson and Bob Chatsworth sat on one side of the conference table. Their top security officer Elliot Thomason sat on the other side with two of his security officers- Larry Addison and Peter Williams.

The head of the firm Tom Berenger said, "Elliot I need you to look at something." He got up and turned off the lights. He pressed the play button on the recorder. There was a recording of my father going through unauthorized records in a file room that he was never to have access to.

"Something is going to have to be done about Weber," Larry Addison said. "We can't afford to let that information get out to the media or the government. Those bastards would love to shut us down and put us away for the next twenty years."

"What do you think he will do with the information?" Elliot Thomason asked.

"What the hell do you think he wants with it?" Bob Chatsworth asked angrily. "He wants to destroy us. He's a fucking boy scout. After everything this firm has done for that bastard he does this to us? I'm not going to lose everything I have worked for all these years for that self-righteous son-of-a-bitch!"

"What do you want us to do?" asked Elliot.

"What we need you to do we can't say out loud now can we?" Tom asked slyly. "Elliot I can't stress the importance of getting rid of this threat. This type of situation is exactly what you're paid to handle. There can be no mistakes. Just get the job done."

Elliot Thomason and Tom Berenger stared into each others eyes. Tom Berenger told him what needed to be done without saying a word. His eyes did the talking for him. Elliot Thomason nodded his head in acknowledgement. He and the two security officers with him got up and left the conference room. They were nothing more than a killing squad. They were on a mission to stop my father from turning over incriminating evidence that could potentially destroy the law firm.

My father had made up his mind to turn over all the evidence he had gathered to Federal Agents the next evening after work. He had already notified them and they had arranged for a secret rendezvous on the other side of Miami Beach at ten o'clock at night. My father called my mother around nine o'clock and told her that he had a late business dinner to attend with potential clients and that he would be home very late. He told her not to wait up for him and that he loved her very much. My mother didn't know it, but that was the last conversation she would ever have with her husband. He continued on his journey to meet with the Federal Agents. He never made it. He noticed that a car was behind him once he got on the Venetian Bridge leading to Miami Beach. My father still didn't know that his law associates were on to him so he thought nothing of it. Suddenly, the car sped up and bumped his car. My father pulled over on the bridge. He reached in the glove compartment and pulled out his car insurance information. The security officers from my father's law firm, Larry Addison and Peter Williams got out of their car. They walked up to the passenger and the driver's side of my father's car.

My father recognized them. He smiled and said, "Hey....."

Before he could say another word each of them pulled out a sawed off shot gun and pointed them at my father's head. When they aimed their guns at my father he was stunned. He couldn't believe what was happening. They shot my father to death right there on the bridge leading to Miami Beach. They each put several bullets into my father's head which was your typical traditional hit. They were instructed to make sure he didn't survive. They accomplished their murderous task. My father's wounds were of course fatal. Blood poured from his head wounds. Blood and brain fragments splattered all over the inside of my father's car. The shots that entered my father's body shattered his skull, his eye sockets and his jaw. Several bullets also went into both his left and right sides. Even though he was already dead, they kept firing bullet after bullet into his lifeless body. My father slumped over into the driver's side of his car as he took his last breath. His life had ended. The love of our life was gone forever. It was a horrific and bloody scene and a very brutal murder.

The head security officer from my dad's law firm Elliot Thomason drove their car into my father's car and pushed it over the bridge into the water beneath. The car sunk to the bottom of the river. My father was already dead at that time. The three men sped off before the police arrived. The police and the Feds had no concrete evidence as to who the culprits were but they all had an idea. Without witnesses or evidence there was nothing that could be done. There was no DNA evidence, fingerprints or any witnesses to the murder. My father's murder remains an unsolved mystery even today. The police investigation into my father's death yielded no results. In fact, except for tire marks and bullet casings which weren't traced back to anyone, there was no concrete forensic evidence whatsoever. The case went cold. The Feds never showed up at my father's murder scene. Since my father never gave them any incriminating information it wasn't a federal case. They had to remain undercover so that they could find another traitor to turn over evidence to bring down the crooked law firm. Their operations had to remain secret. They let the local police handle the matter. At my father's funeral several days after the autopsy was performed by the medical examiner, his law firm associates and the partners all had the gall to show up. They acted as though they had no knowledge whatsoever as to who ordered the hit on my father or who the murdering culprits were. We also had no idea of their role in my father's murder. We never suspected any of them and they knew it.

"Eleanor if there is anything that any of us at the law firm can do for you and your family please let us know," Larry Addison said unconvincingly. "We are there for you and you know that. Your husband would want us to be."

"Come here Eleanor," Bob Chatsworth said with fake compassion. He gave her a hug in order to try and comfort her. His comfort was insincere.

"I hope the police catch the bastards that did this to your husband," Tom said innocently. "He was a good, good man and was well respected among the partners and other associates." My mother was so distraught that her entire body trembled uncontrollably.

"Oh Eleanor," Tom said. "Come here dear."

He also gave her a hug in order to try and comfort her. All of these men were acting concerned when in actuality they didn't give a damn about any of us. Elliot Thomason used this opportunity to try and search for answers from my mother. He wanted to find out if she had received or heard any incriminating information from my father that could destroy them all.

"Eleanor do you have any idea who could have done this thing to your husband?" Elliot had the nerve to ask. "Did your husband say anything to you before he was murdered?"

"No," she responded. "He didn't say anything to me. He had no enemies that I know of. Everyone loved and respected him. He never did anything to anyone. There was no reason for someone to end his life like this. I don't understand any of this. He was a good man. He was a great husband and a good father. Who could have done such a thing? Who?"

Elliot continued with his interrogation. "Did your husband give you anything," he asked insistently. "Did he give you any documents or maybe a disk of some sort? Think back carefully Eleanor. This is very important. I am only trying to help. If you turn over any information to me it could only help in the location of the killers."

"No," she responded with frustration. "He didn't give me anything. If he would have given me anything I would have turned it over to the police immediately. He gave me nothing."

"Ok. Ok," Larry Addison said. "That's enough Elliot. She obviously doesn't know anything. If she did I'm sure she wouldn't hesitate to tell us first. Wouldn't you Eleanor?"

"Yes of course I would."

"Eleanor wouldn't keep anything from us because she knows that we are only trying to help her and the police find her husband's killers," Tom Berenger said. "She knows that she can trust us and that our security team is the best at handling such a situation. Eleanor if you think of anything call Elliot personally. Call him before you even think of calling the police. We loved your husband as a brother and we can do a much better job at solving this case than the police. They really don't give a damn about your husband. He's nothing more than a statistic to them. Remember, call Elliot first. Alright? Elliot, give her your card."

Elliot reached in his jacket pocket and took a business card out. He handed it to her and said, "Remember call me first. I'll handle this investigation myself."

"Yes," she whispered. She began to cry again. For a very long time my mother was numb with grief. My father was lost to us forever. I never saw him again. I never got to say goodbye. I just pray that my father spends eternity in heaven with the angels surrounding and comforting him. And I pray that he knows that I will always love him.

After awhile Anthony returned home. When he heard my mother's voice coming from the kitchen he cursed underneath his breath. She was the last person he wanted to see. She didn't take shit from anyone. She had been through too much bullshit in this life. The bullshit she endured gave her strength. I wish I had her strength. He walked into the kitchen and looked at her uneasily. He looked at the two of us and mumbled something nasty underneath his breath. To him my mother was nothing more than a bitch and he hated her. To her he was nothing more than a low life asshole. She hated him right back. Anthony had a phony smile on his face.

"Eleanor," he said callously.

My mom looked at him angrily and responded, "Anthony."

"I'll fix you a snack honey," I said uneasily. "You didn't eat anything this morning. You must be hungry. Mom, can I fix you something?"

She stared angrily at Anthony and said, "No. For some reason, I just lost my appetite. Isn't that strange? I was hungry a minute ago. Something or someone has made me sick to my stomach." If he was any closer to her she could possibly have spit in his face.

Anthony stared back at her angrily. You could see the anger and fury in his eyes. He knew that she was referring to him. At that moment he could have actually killed her if he knew he could get away with it. In his mind he couldn't even begin to comprehend how a mere woman could be so daring as to speak in his presence that way. After all, he was the man and it was her place to bow down to him and kiss his ass. He felt this way about all women.

I walked over to the refrigerator and took out some bread, mayonnaise and turkey slices so that I could fix him a sandwich. I closed my eyes for a second, inhaled and prayed that they wouldn't kill each other right there in my kitchen. My mother was notoriously confident in herself and stern. So was he. At that moment it was like a mental battle between man and woman was happening. Anthony did not scare her nor she him. Anthony sat down at the kitchen table across from her and lit a cigarette. My mom took out one of her cigarettes and searched in her purse for her lighter. Anthony reached across the table so that he could light her cigarette with his lighter. She ignored him. She pulled out her own lighter and lit her own cigarette. She wanted nothing from him and she wanted him to know it. She looked up at him with an expression of knowing. She wanted him to know just by looking into her eyes that she had been in this world for a very long time and knew a dog when she saw one. She wasn't fooled by him by any means.

He looked at her with an evil expression on his face in an attempt to intimidate and lower her self-image. She was not moved or afraid. She looked back at him defiantly with an expression of total disgust. She saw him as a formidable opponent. He was puzzled that this mere woman wasn't frightened of him and that she refused to back down emotionally. After all, to him all women were beneath him.

He was thinking to himself, "Who the hell does this bitch think she is?"

What he didn't realize was that my mother had been there before in previous relationships that were emotionally and physically abusive and had decided years earlier to never let a man take away her dignity ever again. Anthony got up and stormed out of the kitchen and left the house. He slammed the front door behind him. I was a nervous wreck. My mother smiled to herself with a feeling of accomplishment at his mental defeat. She put her cigarette out, got up and walked over to me.

I was still fixing Anthony some food to eat even though he had stormed out of the house. She placed her hand over my hands and whispered, "He's gone honey. You don't have to serve him now. Throw it away baby. Throw it away and throw him away. Let him go honey. Let him go before he destroys your entire life and that of my precious grandson. Leave him before it's too late. Well, I've said my peace. There is nothing more I can do. It's all up to you now. I know you'll do the right thing for yourself and my grandson just as I had to do many years ago. I let them all go and that's how I was able to meet your father. If you don't let this one go you could be missing out on the one true love of your life. You will find the right man for you. But honey, Anthony isn't the one." She kissed me on my right cheek and said, "I'll see you later baby." After my mother finished expressing her strong disapproval of my relationship with Anthony she left. After she left my house I cried.

Anthony was determined to put my mother in her place and let her know that she was beneath a man. He decided to hurt her physically. My mother was sixty-two years old and didn't have a lot of strength. One evening as she returned from the grocery store she had an uneasy feeling that someone was following her. She had a handful of groceries. She turned around but no one was there. She continued on to her condominium. She entered the building and walked into the elevator. Just as the elevator was about to close someone stuck their hand through and stopped it from closing shut. It was

Anthony. He was wearing a ski mask. My mother couldn't tell who it was. My mother gasped when she saw the strange man with a ski mask over his face. She became terrified. Fear gripped her heart.

"What do you want?" she yelled out in total terror. "I have money. You can take it all. Please don't hurt me."

She started to scream for help. No one heard her. The elevator door closed. Anthony rushed over to her and punched her in the face. He refused to relinquish his power over to her. He wanted her to feel his physical strength in order to lift up the low self-esteem he had for himself. To me, he was nothing more than a fucking coward! She dropped her bags of groceries as she fell to the elevator floor. She had never felt such excruciating pain before in her life. She folded her body up into the fetal position like a baby in hopes that the man would stop beating her. It didn't work. His heart had no capacity for love or compassion. It was already filled up with hatred and anger for all women. The man felt no sympathy for her. In fact, she could sense his rage. She felt within her heart that she was going to die. She whispered in her heart, "Goodbye my daughters and my beautiful grandson. I'll see you in heaven."

Anthony had actually convinced himself that she was the provocateur of the attack and that she deserved to be beat. He lifted her head up and beat her over and over with his fist. He punched her in the face, the head and the chest. With each punch, tears rolled down her cheeks. Blood was everywhere. My mother's blood even splattered all over Anthony's shirt and shoes. My mother's face and neck had multiple bruises, cuts and abrasions all over it and her face was covered with blood. He even broke her nose. There was so much blood on her face she was barely recognizable. Anthony had beaten her as though she was a man. He had put her in her place and showed her that she was no match against a man. My mother lay on the elevator floor like a wounded little girl. She lost consciousness. Ladies, how would you feel in your heart and soul if this was your mother? How much hatred would you have for the bastard that did this to her? Now you know exactly how I feel.

The elevator door opened and Anthony rushed out before anyone could see him. He ran down the stairs of the building and rushed out the door. There was no one in the lobby at that time so he was able to escape without anyone seeing him. He still had gloves on so his fingerprints were nowhere. He took his cap and gloves off once outside and pushed them into his pocket. He stopped running and began walking down the street innocently as though nothing had happened. He felt exhilarated and full of joy. He felt a real sense of accomplishment at the hell he had put my mother through. He had taken her dignity away and lowered her self-esteem. He did what he set out to do. He set out to destroy her. After all, to him she was nothing but a mere woman. To him she was nothing more than a bitch that was expendable. Anthony jumped into his car and sped off. He went home to clean himself up. As he took a shower he smiled. He was excited at his accomplishment. He had destroyed a woman. My son and I were not home at the time and he knew it. Anthony washed away all evidence of him ever being anywhere near my mother's condominium. There were also no witnesses to him ever leaving our home or entering hers. We knew that Anthony was emotionally abusive to me and Tommy but we had no idea that he was capable of beating up a sixty-year-old woman. What a fucking coward! Beating up a sixty-year-old woman made him feel invincible? Ladies, how sick is that? He threw his bloody clothes into the washing machine to wash away any evidence of the horror he put my mother through so that he could never be held accountable. She was found by a neighbor lying unconscious on the elevator floor. Her friend and neighbor Ms. Frances Williams screamed when she saw my mother laying on the elevator floor covered with blood.

She pushed the elevator stop button and screamed, "Eleanor! Eleanor! Oh God! Someone help! Call the police! Call the police!"

Several neighbors on that particular floor heard her screams and rushed out of their apartments to see what all the commotion was about. Ms. Helena Jacobs, Mr. Edward Ellington, Mr. Joseph Jamison and Mrs. Willona Scottsdale all ran out of their apartments and gathered around the elevator. Mrs. Scottsdale had a broom in her hand and Ms. Helena Jacobs had a butcher knife in hers to use as weapons if needed. All of the neighbors gasped when they saw my mother lying unconscious. All of them were terrified. Nothing this bad had ever happened in their building before. They had always considered themselves to be safe. They did not feel safe anymore. They all now knew that something like this could happen to any of them. For the first time in their lives they all felt vulnerable. Their peace of mind and sense of security was gone.

"Oh dear," Mr. Joseph Jamison said with great concern. "I'll call the police." He pulled out his cell phone and called the police and emergency fire rescue.

"Is she still alive?" Ms. Helena Jacobs asked.

"I think so," Mrs. Scottsdale said cautiously. "It looks like she's still breathing."

"Maybe we should turn her over," Mr. Joseph Jamison said.

"No!" Ms. Helena Jacobs said with great concern. "We can't move her. We don't know how badly she's hurt. We could cause more damage. Wait until fire rescue arrives. They'll know what to do."

Mrs. Scottsdale bent down and wiped my mother's mouth gently with a tissue to get some of the blood off of her face. None of them knew what else to do. Thank God that she was still breathing and her heart was still beating so she didn't need cardiopulmonary resuscitation to be performed by any of them. It didn't take long for help to arrive. Several police squad cars and two emergency fire rescue trucks arrived within minutes of receiving the phone call that a woman had been attacked in the condominium. My mother was barely breathing by the time they arrived. She was in critical condition but she was still alive. The highly trained emergency rescue paramedics used their skills to save my mother's life right at the crime scene before they transferred her to the hospital. Because of her age and health issues they not only had to deal with her trauma but her cardiac problems as well. She had a bad heart due to cardiac arrhythmia and it would take all of their skills to keep her alive. They immediately started an intravenous line on my mother's right arm and gave her oxygen to save her life. My mother was rushed to the intensive care unit at the nearest hospital and remained there for several days before being transferred to the medical surgery floor for recovering after life-saving surgery. She stayed in the hospital for a total of two weeks before finally being released. The police questioned all of my mother's neighbors and searched the entire building for the culprit or culprits who had done this to her. The neighbors didn't know anything and there were no culprits to be found. The camera in the lobby of my mother's building was broken and the manager hadn't had time to have it repaired yet. The police had no witnesses or evidence as to who had committed this horrific act on my mother.

When she first arrived at the hospital the emergency response team rushed over to her to try and do whatever they could to save her life. She was kept on oxygen at 3L/min. The blood was wiped off her body so they could see the extent of the damage. Lab work and x-rays were ordered immediately. Ellen and I were notified by the police of my mother's vicious attack. We were both in shock. We couldn't believe that after everything my mother had been through in life she had to endure such a brutal attack. She didn't deserve this. She deserved more respect than this. I hated the man or men who did this to her. I hated this evil world of ours. I hated all the criminals out in the world who were destroying our lives each and every day. Ellen, Tommy and I rushed over to the hospital. We ran up to the nurse's desk and demanded to know where my mother was. Nurse Colleen told us that my mother was in intensive care and that only the immediate family could see her. We told her that we were her daughters and wanted to see her right away. They wouldn't let Tommy in to see her. He was too young. One of the nurses agreed to keep an eye on him for me. We cried when we saw the condition our mother was in.

The blood had been washed off but her face was swollen. Her eyes, lips and cheeks looked like she had been in a boxing ring with a heavy weight boxer and that he had beat the shit out of her. Seeing my mother like that was one of the most horrific moments of my life. Her x-rays revealed that she had a broken nose, a broken jaw and a concussion besides her busted lip and the multiple abrasions all over her body. She was rushed in for surgery to repair her broken nose and jaw, with Ellen and my authorizations. It was a close call but my mother survived. She was a stronger woman than any of had imagined. She could not tell the police who the culprit was. She never saw his face. We took turns staying at my mother's hospital bedside. We didn't want to leave her alone without family for one second. Both Ellen and I both wanted to protect her. We both felt that we had somehow failed her. After all, we were her daughters and therefore responsible for her safety.

I sat at my mother's bedside and watched as narcotic medication dripped into her delicate little arm through the intravenous line to control her pain and suffering. She was also receiving intravenous antibiotics to fight infection. It tore me up inside to know that she had to endure such hell and I wasn't there to protect her. Just at that moment a physician, Dr. Mannington came into her hospital room. He had her chart in his hands and a Nurse named Debbie at his side.

"How are you feeling today," he asked my mother.

"I'm feeling a lot better doctor and the pain is minimal."

"When can my mother go home?" I asked. "When is she going to be discharged?"

"I have good news. Your mother's wounds are healing nicely. There are no signs of permanent damage. The infection to the wound on her left arm is being controlled by antibiotic therapy and her pain is being controlled by narcotic pain relieving medication. We're going to discontinue her intravenous medications and switch her to medications by mouth. If she continues to respond as well as she is, she can be discharged tomorrow." We were both very relieved.

"Thank you doctor," my mom said.

"Thank you doctor, "I said gratefully. "My sister will be in to help my mother leave the hospital once she is discharged. I have to work tomorrow but my sister Ellen is free. She'll be here early to take my mother home. My mother won't be returning to her own home. She will be staying with my sister indefinitely."

"That's fine," the doctor responded. "I'll alert the social worker immediately so she can help your sister make arrangements for physical therapy and any other support that your sister may need in caring for your mother. We all want her transition back home to be as smooth as possible. We're very sorry this happened to you and we want you to know that this hospital is here to support you with whatever you need." Both the doctor and his nurse left the room.

After my mother was released from the hospital she did refuse to go home. She didn't feel safe anymore. She had no idea if the strange man would return and beat her again in the elevator. She was also having nightmares about being attacked or eaten alive by lions. Her nightmares were becoming strange. She felt as though she was losing her sanity. Ellen and I were both worried about her. She moved in with Ellen as my sister had demanded. My mother had become afraid. Her insecurities about men returned. She also began to feel powerless against them. Thanks to Anthony she lost her self confidence again.

I didn't have to work on the day that my mother was released from the hospital as I had told the doctor. It was a lie. The truth of the matter is that my sister and I weren't talking to each other anymore. Even before my mother had a chance to be released from the hospital all hell broke loose. Anthony destroyed my relationship with my only sister. My sister Ellen was my rock. Whenever I needed her for something she was always there for me and Tommy. She loved Tommy to death and would do anything for him. I could count on her for anything. After Anthony had attacked my mother and alienated all my friends from me he went to work on Ellen. She would come over to see me and he would treat her like shit.

He would ask her stupid questions like, "You here again? Don't you have a life of your own? Don't you have a home of your own?"

Ellen knew he was drunk when he acted like this and besides she wasn't scared of Anthony nor was he able to intimidate her. He knew her strength and he hated her for it. She knew this and flaunted her womanhood and her power in his face every chance that she got. Besides my mother, she was the only other woman that he couldn't control. There was no way he was going to keep her away from her sister or nephew. Ellen wouldn't allow him to do it. Ellen would tell him in a second to go screw himself. Anthony was determined to get Ellen out of our lives. He constantly tried to think of ways to get rid of her. Then one day he got his wish. He executed a plan to destroy the reputation of my sister and destroy our relationship. His plan caused me to completely exclude her from my life and that of my son. He made a complete fool out of me at the expense of my sister. Ellen thought I was home one afternoon so she came over to see if I wanted to get out of the house and go shopping with her. She didn't know that I had taken Tommy for a quick trip to the grocery store to buy some food. She knocked on the door and Anthony opened it.

"What do you want?" he asked.

"Get out of my way asshole," she replied angrily. She pushed him out the way forcefully and then stormed into the house. He smiled sarcastically to himself at her gall. He was amused.

"Where are my sister and nephew?"

"Well, let me see. They could be anywhere. Maybe they're in China. Maybe they're in Japan. Maybe they're on an Alaskan cruise. Or, maybe I just killed the both of them and buried their bodies in the backyard. You never know," he said evilly. He was trying to torment her. His plan was beginning to work.

"If you ever hurt my sister or my nephew I'll hunt you down like the dog you are. There won't be any place on this entire fucking planet where you can hide," she responded angrily.

Anthony laughed at her. Then he stared at her with a look of pure hatred. For the first time, she was afraid.

"I was just kidding," he said slyly. "They're at the grocery store. They'll be right back. You can wait for them. Make yourself at home."

He left her in the kitchen and he went into the downstairs bathroom and took his shirt off. He put some cologne on. As he combed his hair he stared at his reflection in the mirror with a blank look on his face. It was almost as though he was dead inside. Ellen was in the kitchen drinking a glass of water. Anthony left the bathroom and went to the front window by the front door. He peeped out the window to see when I drove up.

When he saw me pull my SUV into the driveway an evil expression came over his face. He slowly walked into the kitchen where Ellen was. As he did, he started to unzip his pants. He walked up behind her and she turned around.

"Anthony, what the fuck do you thing you're doing?" she asked as her fears bean to grow into total terror.

He grabbed Ellen tightly by her arms and fell over backwards, pulling her on top of him. He lifted up her dress and put his right hand between for legs. He held her close to him with his left arm so tightly that she couldn't move. He kissed her on the mouth so forcefully that she couldn't talk or even yell out. She couldn't move. She thought that he was trying to rape her. She was repulsed by his touch. She had no idea that it was all just a set up to destroy our relationship. Just at that moment I walked into the kitchen. Tommy had run upstairs to listen to his music. He never made it into the kitchen and didn't see anything that was going on between my sister and my man. When I saw them 'making out' on the floor my heart dropped. I felt as though someone had taken a knife and stabbed me in the heart. I couldn't breathe. I struggled to catch my breath. I felt breathless. Anthony stopped when he heard me. He pretended like he didn't see me.

"Ellen, I can't do this," he said still pretending to be intoxicated. "I'm drunk and I don't know what's happening here. Why do you want to have sex with me? I thought you hated me. I'm your sister's man. I love her. I thought you loved her too. You're acting like the slut I thought you were."

Ellen slapped Anthony and yelled, "Get off of me you sick bastard!"

Anthony said anything he could to incriminate my sister and I bought into his lies. He looked at me and said, "Michelle I didn't know you were back. Look, don't be mad at her. She loves you. She just got a little carried away. Don't hate her."

Michelle and I were both crying.

"Michelle he's lying," Ellen screamed. "He pulled me on top of him. You know me. You know I don't want this stink alcoholic bastard touching me. You have to believe me. I'm your sister. I love you."

I started screaming at Ellen. I told her to get out the fuck out of my house.

"Ellen don't give me that I love you bullshit," I yelled. "Anthony wasn't on top of you. You were on top of him with your dress pulled up. You are nothing but a slut! I thought I could trust you. You've always been jealous of me and Anthony. That's why you act like you hate him. The truth of the matter is you've always wanted him. You couldn't go out and get your own man. You had to try and steal mine."

I walked over to Ellen and slapped her in the face so hard I left my hand print in her face. She slapped me back in my face. Anthony was very pleased. His plan was working terrifically.

"I can't believe you're gonna take his word over mine," she yelled. "You are a stupid bitch! I hope he kills your ass. I will never forgive you for this Michelle. I will never forgive either of you."

As she started to storm out of the house Tommy who had heard all the fuss ran down the stairs and asked, "What's wrong Aunt Ellen? What happened?"

She ignored him and stormed out of the house.

"Tommy get back to your room," I yelled. Get back upstairs now."

Tommy ran back upstairs. He was totally confused. He didn't understand what was happening. Anthony, pretending like he was still drunk, stumbled and zipped up his pants.

"I don't know what happened," he said in an unconvincingly intoxicated slurred voice. "I got to cut down on my drinking so if something like this happens again I can handle it better. I'm gonna stop drinking for you; for us. I'm sorry you had to find out what a slut your sister is. I tried to tell you before but you wouldn't listen to me. Now maybe you'll start believing what I say."

I didn't want to hear anymore from Anthony or Ellen. I couldn't talk. I had nothing to say. I just went upstairs and checked on my son.

Tommy asked, "Mom what happened to Aunt Ellen? Why was she crying?"

"Don't worry honey," I said softly. "Your mom and your Aunt Ellen had a fight, that's all. Everything is going to be ok."

I went to my room and cried myself to sleep. Anthony who was very pleased with himself and the way things turned out went into the living room and made his self a drink. He had deliberately lied to me and made a fool out of me and my sister.

"The bitch is not a bad piece," he whispered sarcastically to himself. "I should have tapped that ass a long time ago."

My mother was finally ready to be discharged from the hospital. A registered nurse named Ashley came into the room to check my mother's vital signs. She smiled after checking my mother's temperature, pulse and blood pressure.

"Ms. Weber it looks like you're being sprung from the hospital today," she said comfortingly. "The doctor says that you are stable enough to go home. Isn't that great?"

My mother smiled and said, "Yes. I want to get out of here. But I'm not going home. I can't go back there yet. I'm too frightened."

"I understand Ms Weber, Nurse Ashley said with concern. "Are you going to stay with one of your daughters?"

"Yes. I'm staying with my daughter Ellen. She's going to look after me. Well, both of my daughters are going to be caring for me."

Just at that moment Ellen walked into the hospital room.

"Hello mom. How are you feeling? Are you in pain? Do you feel strong enough to get out of here?"

"I feel strong enough baby. I'm ready to get out of here now. Where's your sister? How come she didn't come?"

"She went to work. She'll see you later at my place. Don't worry. She's bringing your grandson with her. You'll get to see both of them soon. Hello nurse."

"Hello Ms. Weber," Ashley responded back. "Your mother has been cleared for release by the doctor. Here are her release papers and some instructions from the doctor. I want you to read everything and then sign. Make sure your mother follows the doctor's instructions carefully and takes all of her medications as instructed. Let me know if you have any questions. Ok?"

"Thank you," Ellen said.

"I'll be right back," Ashley said. "I have to get your mother's prescriptions. The doctor has ordered several medications for her to take. I'll be right back to explain everything to you."

The nurse left the room. Ellen read the documents and signed where the nurse told her to.

"Mom thanks for agreeing to stay at my place instead of going back home. We don't feel comfortable with you going back to your place this soon after the attack. I know you're still frightened, but Michelle and I will take care of you. Don't worry about anything. You'll be safe with me. There is no way you're going to Michelle's place. That asshole Anthony is there. The last thing you need is to deal with that stupid bitch and her asshole drunken bastard man."

My mother was shocked at the way Ellen was speaking about me. "Why are you talking so nasty against your own sister?" she asked with concern. "You two love each other. What has gotten you so mad at her?"

She didn't want to worry my mother so she just played it off. She pretended as though nothing was wrong.

She smiled and said, "Nothing mom. I'm just mad at Anthony. He got a little drunk and showed his ass. That's all. Everything is going to be alright. I don't want you to worry about anything right now. You need to get your strength back. Let's just go on to my place. Come on. Let's get out of here."

The nurse came back into the room. "Ms Weber the doctor has ordered you to take some pain pills as needed," she instructed. "When your pain comes back just follow the doctor's orders as written on the physician's orders. Also, Doctor Miller has ordered some antibiotics for you to fight infection and some anti-inflammatory medication to help with the swelling. You must follow the doctor's orders as written. Please complete the antibiotics until every pill is finished. Some people take some of the antibiotics and then just stop when they feel better. In order to benefit from the medication regime you have to take every pill as ordered by the doctor. Don't stop until they are all complete. Also, the doctor would like to see you as an outpatient in his office in two weeks to check on your status. Ok?"

"Yes. I will follow the doctor's orders as written."

"Do either of you have any questions?"

My mother and Ellen both said no. The nurse helped my mother into a wheelchair and wheeled her to the elevator. They rode in the elevator down to the lobby and outside. Ellen went to get the car and drove it to the entrance of the hospital. They helped my mother into the car and Ellen drove away. My mother stayed with Ellen for several weeks. As for Ellen and me, we didn't talk to each other during those weeks. I was hurt by her and she was disappointed in me. I would go over to see my mother when Ellen wasn't home. I didn't want my mother to get mixed up in our drama. She had been through enough. But, like I said before, my mother had been on this earth a lot of years and she knew more than either of her daughters could imagine. She was no fool. She knew in her spirit that something was wrong. She knew her daughters. She stayed silent and waited for us to work it out amongst ourselves. She wanted to see just what her daughters were made of. She wanted to see if what she had taught her daughters over the years meant anything to us. She wanted to see if we had the capacity to forgive and understand. She wanted to see the essence of who her daughters were.

Things got worst after the Ellen incident. Anthony was distancing himself further and further away from Tommy and me. He was having alcoholic induced hallucinations. He was becoming paranoid and began to believe that everyone was against him. Everyone on the planet earth had become his enemy. To escape the situation, I also began to withdraw more and more. Tommy himself began to act out from all the tension at home. He was getting into trouble at school again and getting detention over and over again. Ladies, can you blame him? This was a lot for a young man to deal with. It wasn't fair to him. There were even threats from his principal for him to get suspended. The drama in the house increased dramatically. Anthony was becoming angrier and would blow up over the littlest things. Nothing I did pleased him anymore and Tommy was really getting on his nerves. One day Tommy had left his baseball on the floor near the front door of the house. It was Friday night and of course Anthony had been drinking. Anthony came home later that evening and opened the front door. He was drunk of course and he stumbled into the house. He tripped over Tommy's baseball and fell to the floor.

"Got dammit!" he yelled. "Who the hell left this stuff on the floor? I could've broken my neck. Tommy, get your stupid little ass down here. I'm gonna whip your ass."

I ran out into the hallway to see what was going on and there he was. He was sitting on the floor and yelling out like a maniac.

"Anthony, why are you yelling out like that?" I asked with concern. "The whole neighborhood could hear you? Tommy is asleep now. What are you doing here on the floor?" As I helped him up I could smell the liquor on his breath.

He asked with a slurred voice as he stood up, "What do you mean what am I doing on the floor? It was your stupid son. What's his name? Tommy. That kid left his ball on the floor and I fell down. Tommy, get up! I'm gonna whip your ass." In his drunken stupor he was talking incoherent gibberish.

"Shush," I whispered. "Anthony, stop now. Don't wake Tommy up. He's exhausted and he needs his rest. He's just a kid."

Anthony yelled in his drunken stupor, "I don't give a damn who he is. I'm still gonna whip him for leaving this stuff all over the floor."

"Anthony I'll pick up his ball," I pleaded. I picked Tommy's ball up off the floor. Anthony became more furious. He looked at me with an expression of pure evil.

"Are you gonna take his ass whipping as well?" he asked angrily. "That's fine with me. That works for me you stupid worthless bitch."

Anthony slapped me with the back of his hand so hard that I fell against the wall. He actually left his hand print in my face. He busted my lip open and blood squirted out. He rushed up to me and grabbed my hair so hard that I thought he was going to pull it right out of my scalp.

"Anthony, please stop." I cried out. Please! You're hurting me."

"Oh, I'm hurting you," he screamed. "If you ever fuck with me like this again I'll really show you what hurt is you stupid bitch."

He pushed me up against the wall and then he let my hair go. I slid to the floor out of fear. He went upstairs and went into the bathroom. He kneeled over the toilet and tried to vomit in it. He missed and most of the vomit landed on the bathroom floor and against the wall. I could hear him from all the way downstairs. After he finished he went into our bedroom, threw himself across the bed and passed out. That was the first time Anthony had hit me. But, it wouldn't be the last. I wasn't only hurt physically, but mentally as well. I loved this man and couldn't understand why he was treating me so badly. "What did I do wrong?" I asked myself.

I started to question myself as a woman and felt like all the problems Anthony and I were having was my own fault. I slowly got off the floor and walked into the downstairs bathroom and washed the blood from my face. I grabbed a small hand towel from the linen closet and went into the kitchen. I opened the freezer door, took some ice cubes and placed them in the hand towel. I took the hand towel filled with ice into the living room and laid it on the coffee table. I went upstairs to Tommy's room where he was asleep. I walked over to his bed, helped him out of bed and walked him downstairs with me. He was half asleep as he walked. There was no way in hell that I would let my child sleep upstairs with that drunken bastard that night. I walked over to the couch with my son and we sat down. He laid his head on my lap as I reached over to the coffee table and picked up the hand towel with ice in it. I placed the hand towel to my lips to help the swelling go down. The entire side of my face where Anthony had hit me hurt so badly it felt like someone had beat me with a hammer. My son was with me so I was trying to fight back the tears. Tommy must have awakened during the night and went to the other couch because the next morning he wasn't near me any more. Anthony came down and apologized for slapping me.

"Michelle I have never laid my hand on a woman before," he said innocently. "I'm so sorry. I swear I'll never, ever lift a finger to hurt you again. And I love Tommy. You must know that I would never do anything to hurt him." He hugged me gently and looked at my busted lip.

"Shit!" he said with fake concern. "I can't believe I did that. Oh my God. I'm so sorry. I'm going to fix all this. You'll see. Everything is going to be alright." The 'Honeymoon Phase' in an abusive relationship was all this was. It was fake and deceiving. It meant nothing. "Are you going to be ok?"

"Yes, I'll be ok," I replied. In reality I wasn't alright. I was hurt physically and emotionally. I was scared for myself and my child. I didn't know what to do. Tommy woke up and got off the couch.

He walked over to me and asked, "Mom what happened to your mouth?"

Anthony quickly answered, "Your mom fell down. She's ok though. I'm here with her and I'll take care of her needs. Ok? You get yourself ready for school now. The bus will be here at any moment."

Tommy looked at me with a concerned expression on his face but he did what Anthony had asked. He went upstairs to wash up and get dressed for school. I started out for the kitchen to fix him some cereal for breakfast, but Anthony stopped me.

"No, no. You don't have to do anything this morning. You go into the living room, put your feet up and I'll fix Tommy something to eat. I'll even bring you in a hot cup of coffee and Danish like you like. How about it? Ok?"

He was feeling guilty about the way he had treated me and in a vain attempt at trying to make me feel better was allowing me to rest. I shook my head "yes" and I walked into the living room and sat down. Anthony went into the kitchen and fixed breakfast for all of us. He was humming and singing as though nothing had happened. His nonchalant attitude was like rubbing salt on an open wound. It was insulting and disrespectful. Tommy came downstairs a short time later and sat to the kitchen table to eat his cereal. Anthony brought me in my coffee and Danish. He went back to the kitchen table with Tommy and sat down with him.

He stared at Tommy for a few minutes and then asked, "Tommy did you know you left your baseball on the floor last night by the doorway and I almost hurt myself? Do you remember when you did that before and I told you that if I caught it on the floor again I was going to throw it in the garbage?"

Tommy looked at Anthony with a terrified look on his face.

"Yes Anthony," he said fearfully. "I'm sorry. It won't happen again."

I heard the conversation and I got up and went into the kitchen.

"Come on honey," I said with concern. "The school bus will be here soon. Let's get you ready for school."

Thank god that at that exact moment the school bus driver honked his horn and Tommy rushed out the door to go to school. As he rushed out I gave him his book bag and some lunch money.

"Bye mom. Bye Anthony," Tommy yelled as he ran out the door to head for school.

Anthony looked at me with an angry expression and said, "I have to get ready for work. Maybe you should take the day off, you know with that busted lip of yours. You don't want your co-workers asking a lot of stupid questions."

He was right. I couldn't let any of my co-workers see my face busted up like it was. I didn't want people asking me a lot of questions or whispering about me behind my back.

"Yes. I think I will call in sick today and tomorrow," I responded. "I haven't taken any time off in awhile. I'm due."

Anthony said in a nonchalant voice, "I'll be home early tonight. How about you make some pork chops and baby peas for dinner? I love that shit. I'll see you later. Get some rest today."

He walked out the door and headed for work as though nothing had happened. He was pretending as though we had the perfect relationship and that everything was fine. I guess to him a man beating a woman was no big deal. He was acting as though I was one of his buddies that he had gotten into a fight with. He was acting like it was ok for a man to hit a woman because 'boys will be boys.' His attitude was just as insulting as the physical act itself. After Anthony and Tommy had left the house I called my job and spoke to my supervisor Jennifer Jones. I explained to her that I wasn't feeling well and needed a couple of sick days.

"It must be that flu that's going around," Jennifer said with genuine concern. "Everyone is getting it. I just got over the flu myself. I was sick all of last week. I hope you feel better. Take care of yourself. Don't rush back. The company is not going to fall apart if you take some time off for yourself. Take your time. You have some vacation time left. Use it now. Take care Michelle." She hung up.

I decided to do some cleaning up. I went upstairs and cleaned up the vomit from off the bathroom floor and wall. I washed Anthony's stinky clothes next and proceeded to clean the rest of the house. As I cleaned I couldn't help but wonder about Elaine. She was my sister. I missed her. But, the bitch tried to sleep with my man and I would never forgive her for that.

I put her out of my mind and went on with my housework. When Tommy got home from school he got a snack and then went straight to his room to do his homework. After he finished he went out in the back yard to play with his dog Chucky. I prepared dinner just as Anthony had asked. I didn't want to do anything to make him mad.

After dinner was ready Tommy came back inside and asked, "Mom is dinner ready? I'm starving."

"Yes honey," I said. "Dinner is ready. Go upstairs and wash up. Anthony should be home at any minute."

"Ok mom."

He rushed up the stairs to get ready for dinner. We waited for an hour and Anthony never showed up. I couldn't let Tommy go hungry any longer so I went on and fed him. I didn't eat though because I remembered that Anthony said he wanted to eat together as a family and I figured that he wouldn't get mad if at least I ate with him. I was wrong. Anthony showed up three hours after dinner was ready. He had stopped at the local bar and had a few drinks. He was drunk as usual. You could smell the stench of liquor not only on his breath, but it was permeating out of the pores of his skin.

Tommy was already upstairs in his room watching television and playing with his dog Chucky.

Anthony stumbled into the living room where I was sitting and asked, "Is dinner ready? I'm sorry I'm late. I was just hanging out with a couple of my buddies."

"Yes Anthony," I responded. I was obviously annoyed with him. "Dinner is ready. In fact, it was ready three hours ago. You promised me that you would be home early. You know what, never mind. Let me go and just heat everything up. Go on and wash up. Dinner will be ready soon. Go on."

Anthony went into the downstairs bathroom and freshened up for dinner. He then walked into the living room and fixed himself another drink. He brought it to the dining table with him and joined me for dinner. He took a few slips of the liquor and then started to eat.

He looked around and said, "Where's Tommy? I thought I told you that I wanted to have a family dinner with the three of us."

"Dinner was ready three hours ago Anthony," I replied. "Tommy was hungry so I went on and fed him. He's just a kid. I can't make him wait that long."

Anthony yelled, "What do you mean? He can't what? Who the hell is he? His stupid little ass can wait just like everybody else. You know what, I'm tired of this. You treat that kid like he's a damn baby. He's twelve years old. Not one or two. He's twelve. You know what, forget this and you. This food tastes like garbage anyway." He threw the plate of food across the room and it splattered all over the wall.

I jumped up and said, "Anthony please calm down. Don't get upset like this. We can all eat together tomorrow night. I promise."

"What did you say to me?" he asked angrily.

I could hear the anger in his voice. I had heard that tone before. His violent behavior usually followed it. I became terrified.

"You don't tell me how to act," he yelled. "I'm the damn man of this house and I'll act any way I want to." He jumped up from the table, rushed over to me and slapped me across the face. He slapped me so hard I fell to the floor. Tommy had heard all the yelling and came rushing down the stairs. Our dog Chucky was right behind him barking like crazy.

"You leave my mother alone," Tommy yelled out in total terror. "Stop hitting her. Leave her alone."

Chucky ran over to us and continued to bark. Anthony pushed Chucky away. Chucky whimpered and hid underneath the living room couch.

"I hate you!" Tommy screamed out. "I hate you and I hope you die!"

"What did you just say to me you stupid little bastard?" responded Anthony angrily. He took off his belt and ran after Tommy. Tommy tried to get away but Anthony was too fast for him. Anthony grabbed Tommy by the arm and started beating him with the belt. Ladies, what would you do if an abusive man started beating your child with a belt? He was beating him so hard that he left black and blue marks all over his body. I stopped crying when I saw my child in trouble. I jumped up off the floor and ran to help my son.

As I ran I yelled out, "You leave my son alone you stupid bastard! Leave him alone! I swear I'll kill you for this!"

I ran up behind Anthony and jumped on his back. I was willing to do whatever I had to in order to save my child. He let Tommy go and tried to hit me with his belt. His swing was too wide and he kept missing me. Tommy ran and fell to the floor right in front of Anthony's legs. He reached over and bit Anthony in the shin with his teeth as hard as he could.

Anthony yelled out, "Ouch! Got dammit! You little piece of ...."

He grabbed Tommy and threw him down the hall. He turned around and pushed me into the wall. It felt like he had just broken my back. Every part of my body was hurting. The pain was excruciating. I fell to the floor. Chucky had crawled from underneath the couch and was barking like crazy. Then Anthony decided to go after Tommy again. He snapped the belt like it was a whip and started beating Tommy again. I was in a state of total panic. He was hurting my child and I had to do something even if it meant killing him. I became enraged. I was going on pure adrenaline now. I needed that adrenaline to save my child. How dare this lunatic touch my child. I ran into the living room and grabbed a lamp. I snatched the cord from the wall as hard as I could and carried the lamp to where Anthony was beating Tommy. In my desperation I lifted the lamp up into the air and slammed it into the side of Anthony's head. I tried to bash his brains out.

I realize now that hitting him over the head was foolish and dangerous and could have made the entire situation much more dangerous. But, at the time I was working on clear adrenaline. I wasn't in the right frame of mind. I would never suggest that any other woman on the entire planet earth repeat my actions. Just get out and away ladies. Let the police handle the situation. Find help before you even get into such a dangerous predicament. It will save you years of grief and a possible jail sentence.

He fell over onto the floor in agony. He was holding the side of his head with his hands. His fury was unmistakable.

He was yelling out, "You're going to pay for this. Both of you are going to die tonight. The police are going to drag your bodies out in body bags by the time I finish with you two. The coroner won't be able to identify your bodies by the time I'm done."

Fear gripped the very essence of my soul. He had threatened my child's life. It became clear to me that my son and I were going to die if I didn't do something quickly. The thought of losing my son and having his life end at the hands of that shameless fool was unbearable. The danger that my son was now in was totally my fault. I brought this danger into his life. I led this evil right to him. It was my responsibility that he was in danger and it was now my responsibility to save him. I screamed for help but it was useless. No one heard me. I will never forget my son's eyes and the look of terror he showed me. I had put that fear in my son's heart by bringing this man into his life. I felt shear panic. I grabbed my son, we ran upstairs and I locked us in Tommy's bedroom. Chucky followed us upstairs into the bedroom. I grabbed the phone and called the police. Anthony meanwhile got up off the floor and stumbled into the kitchen. He was bleeding from the side of his head and the side of his face was covered with blood. He grabbed a large sharp butcher's knife from the utensils drawer and headed up the stairs. He had a wild look in his eyes, almost like a mad dog.

All the while he was yelling, "I'm gonna kill you. I'm going to kill you and that bastard son of yours. Hell, I'm even gonna kill your damn dog. You can't hide from me bitch." He ran up the stairs and started banging on the door. Chucky started barking again and Tommy screamed out in fear.

"He's gonna kill us mom." Tommy cried out in terror. "He's gonna kill us. What are we gonna do?"

"Shush honey," I whispered in an attempt to calm my son down. "Don't worry. The police are on their way. They're gonna stop him and he'll never hurt us again. I promise you that." I held my son and tried to comfort him.

Anthony just kept banging and banging on the door while holding the knife up into the air. I was trying to be brave for my son but I had never been so scared in my life. I wasn't scared for myself. I was scared for my son. I would gladly give up my life for him.

"Anthony the police are coming," I yelled out. "Get away from the door! Leave us alone!"

After a few minutes the police arrived. We could hear several squad cars pulling up to the house and policemen jumping out and yelling. Several of them ran around back and several stayed in the front. They yelled out, "This is the police. Come out with your hands up." It was a profound relief to both Tommy and me to hear that the police had finally arrived.

"The police are here mom." Tommy yelled out with excitement.

"I know baby," I responded. "We're safe now. Everything is going to be alright. Anthony can't hurt us now."

Anthony said to himself, "Ah, damn! The police are here. Damn!" He walked downstairs waving the knife into the air like a madman. He stormed out of the house onto the porch holding the knife into the air. He was waving the knife in the air in a threatening way to the police. In his mind someone was going to die that night and he didn't care who it was.

"Get the hell away from my property," Anthony yelled out. "All of you are trespassing. I'll kill every one of you pigs if you don't get the hell out of here."

The police had their guns drawn at this time and were staying a safe distance away from Anthony. They yelled out, "This is the police! Drop the knife! Drop it now!"

The policemen who had went around back, busted down the back door and carefully entered the house. They wanted to make sure that no one else was in the home with a weapon for their safety and that of their fellow officers. When they determined that the downstairs area was safe and that no one was down there two of them headed upstairs. They had their guns drawn and were ready for any surprises. They continued to yell out over and over, "Police! Is anyone here? Put your weapons down and put your hands up!"

When they reached Tommy's locked bedroom door they yelled, "Police! Is anyone in there?"

I yelled, "Yes, me and my son. I'm Michelle and I'm here with my son and his dog."

Officer Jackson asked, "Do you have any weapons? Is anyone hurt?"

I said, "Yes my son Tommy has been beaten and no one has any weapons in here."

Officer Jackson said, "Unlock the door and step all the way back. Make sure you secure your pet."

I unlocked the door and we stepped all the way back. Tommy grabbed hold of Chucky so he wouldn't charge the officers. The cops peaked in and when they determined that they were safe and that we had no weapons they came on in.

Officer Jackson asked, "Mam are you ok? Is either of you hurt?"

I said, "My boyfriend beat my son with a belt. He's hurt."

Officer Richardson said, "Mam we will get your son to the hospital as soon as the situation with your boyfriend outside is under control. It's too dangerous and we don't want either of you to get hurt. Son, are you alright?"

Tommy said, "Yes sir."

Officer Richardson said gently, "Good. Everything is going to be alright. Your mom and you are both safe. Just keep holding the dog. Don't let him go."

"Ok," Tommy promised.

Officer Jackson and Officer Richardson asked me to explain everything that had happened. I told them everything they wanted to know. Then, they escorted us downstairs and told us to sit in the kitchen and stay away from the windows. We left Chucky upstairs and closed him up in the bedroom for his safety.

Meanwhile, outside Anthony decided to push the remaining officers into a situation of murder by cop. The possibility of him being incarcerated had become inevitable. He faced the possibility of being charged with kidnapping, aggravated assault, child abuse, domestic abuse, threatening the safety of police officers, resisting arrest and more. He knew he was going to go to jail. He decided to force them to shoot him. There was no way in hell he was going to spend time in prison. His philosophy was that there was no way he was going to spend time in prison being some man's sex slave. He found the entire situation repulsive. He would rather die first. He lunged forward off the porch with the knife up in the air at one of the officers. Shots rang out and Anthony lay dead on the ground. He had been shot at least twenty-five times by the officers. He posed a clear and present danger to all of them and he had to be taken down. They did what they had to do to prevent injury to themselves and to the public. As the bullets tore through his flesh, he grabbed his stomach and cried out in agony. His eyes rolled in the back of his sockets and he gasped for air. Blood poured from his gunshot wounds of which there were many. The bastard got his wish. He wanted to die so he did.

I didn't shed one tear for him that day. My tears were for my hurt son. He was the only one that mattered to me. I got on my cell phone and called my sister and my mother. I needed them both. I told them to get to the house right away. I told them that Anthony tried to kill me and Tommy.

I begged, "Ellen please, please don't hang up. Anthony's dead. He tried to kill me and Tommy."

She yelled, "What! Where the hell are you two?"

"We're at the house. They shot Anthony. He's dead. There are police everywhere. Please come. We need you."

"We'll be right there. Hold on."

She hung up the phone and came with my mother as quickly as she could. I still can't believe that even after the way I treated her she still had my back. My sister Ellen was my best friend and I abandoned her.

Within thirty minutes my mother and my sister drove up to the house. They jumped out of the car and ran over to us as fast as they could. The police escorted my son and me out of the house.

On the way out of the house I told Tommy, "Close your eyes baby."

He closed his eyes tightly. I didn't want him to see Anthony lying on the ground bleeding so I guided his steps. I was his eyes. Once outside I noticed that Anthony was covered up with a white sheet. I closed my eyes for a second and tried to forget that I even knew the bastard. The police wouldn't let my mom and my sister past the ropes.

Officer Peters yelled, "This is a crime scene. You can't come in here."

I yelled, "That's my mother and my sister."

The police refused to let them inside the crime scene but they did let them come over to me and my son. When we saw each other Ellen, my mom, Tommy and I all started crying. Ellen and I ran up to one another and hugged. I held onto my sister tightly. I didn't want to let her go. When we finished hugging we both looked at each other and started apologizing at the same time.

I cried, "Oh God Ellen. I'm so, so sorry for accusing you of trying to steal Anthony from me. I now know what a conniving bastard he was. I should have trusted and believed in you. Can you ever forgive me?"

She said in a joking way, "Shush! Shut up bitch. Don't worry about anything. I'm here now. Everything is going to be ok."

I had my Ellen back. We smiled at each other. My mom gave Tommy a big hug.

She asked, "Are you ok honey."

He said, "Yeah grandma. I'm ok."

Ellen walked over to Tommy and gave him a big hug.

SEX: With a Cheater, Abuser, Addict

While we were waiting for the ambulance I gave my statement to Officer Frank Washington and Officer Antwain O'Malley and they wrote everything down. At this time a couple of ambulances, fire rescue, crime scene investigators and other officers showed up at the scene. Fire rescue and four ambulance drivers drove up to the house to assess the situation. One of the officers named Lt. Peter Browne called over a couple of paramedics from fire rescue for me and Tommy. They attended to our wounds. After Anthony's was officially pronounced dead and the initial investigation completed, his body was removed and transferred to the medical examiner's office for an autopsy.

One of the paramedics Bobby Elwood said, "Both of you need to be checked out by a physician. Is that alright Mam?"

"Yes," I replied. "I am especially concerned for my son. He has been injured."

When it was determined that we had no serious injuries, the fire rescue crew left us in the care of one of the emergency medical response teams. We were transferred to the hospital for evaluation via ambulance. My mother and sister followed us in their car.

The emergency room physician Dr. Tim Barnes finally came in and examined both of us. His nurse Tanya Peterson joined him. The doctor came into the waiting room wearing his white lab coat. He was very tall and very handsome. I couldn't help but notice how attractive he was. But, at that moment I didn't give a damn if he was the most handsome man on the planet earth. He could have stripped down naked, laid down on a mink rug, poured honey all over his body and invited me to lick him from head to toe in his five million dollar mansion and it would have been of no significance. My son had been hurt and traumatized. He was my one and only priority in life at the moment. God had entrusted this young boy's life in my hands and I swore to myself that I would never neglect my responsibilities as a mother again. I was concerned about not only my son's physical health but his mental health as well. To hell with men! Dr Barnes checked me and Tommy out from head to toe and ordered x-rays to ensure that there were no fractures or internal injuries.

After we got the ok to go home from the doctor Ellen took us all to her home. She said that there was no way that we were going to stay in that house that night. She wanted us to stay where she could keep and eye on the both of us. I closed the house up for several weeks after Anthony was killed. I knew that Tommy was traumatized and couldn't deal with living at our house at that time. We both started intensive psychotherapy and were on the road to recovery. Ellen actually joined us for some of the therapy sessions. She needed to heal too. The two of us were back together. We both made a solemn vow to never leave each other. Ellen and I were sisters again and I swore that I would never let anyone separate us again.

Chapter 4

I'M WRITING THIS letter to all my sisters around the world who have been in a relationship with a man who is addicted to internet porn and is emotionally abusive. I know exactly what you're going through. Ladies, it's not your fault. You are not his mother and he is not a child. He has to face up to his problems and get help for himself. You are not a psychiatrist and you are not equipped to handle his addiction by yourself. He needs professional help and it is up to him to get it. If he won't get help and it is causing you suffering and pain than get out. Get out before his addiction destroys you. Stephen told me over and over that I was his woman and that he owned me. He told me that I was his property and I will do what he tells me to do. I allowed him to pressure me into behavior that I am now ashamed of. I was actually enabling my man to pull me into a world of erotica. Stephen would sit in front of that damn computer every chance he got. I swear ladies, that bastard loved that computer or shall I say the naked bitches on the computer more than he loved me. The women on those X-rated websites had huge fake breasts and were wiling to expose everything that God gave them. They looked like hookers. How could I compete with that? Or, should I ask, "Why the hell should I have to compete with that?" His refusal to give up this lifestyle acted as a catalyst in the total destruction of our relationship. These women were unreal. I tried everything I could think of to please Stephen but he never seemed to be satisfied. I was not enough for him. He wanted more. But he wanted more of what? I don't even think that Stephen knew exactly what he wanted. I realize now that I wasn't the problem. Stephen was the problem. He was addicted to pornography and it destroyed our relationship. It wasn't my fault. I didn't recognize myself any more. I became ashamed of myself and I lost my self-dignity. I stopped going to church. I stopped reading my bible. I stopped praying to God for his guidance. I was not the woman that God had intended me to be. I was better than this. Even though I forgot about God, he never forgot about me. One day when I finally stopped fighting him God brought me back to him. He forgave me for all of my sins and blessed me with eternal life through the blood of Jesus Christ who died for my sins. I had to dig deep down within my soul and find the woman I had forgotten. I had to find myself again. I had to kick Stephen and his porn out of my life. Ladies please do not be my judge and jury. I am not the only one. There are millions of women all over the world just like me. We are as one.

Stephen and I had lived together for over a year in New York City. We met and immediately fell deeply in love. Our attraction for each other was undeniable. It was love at first sight. I had never fallen that deeply or that quickly for another man before. He took my breath away with his sexiness, kindness, compassion and strength. He was the love of my life, or so I thought. New York had always been my home state. I loved everything about New York. I loved the people and their different ethnicities. I loved the different cultures. I loved the night life. I loved the restaurants, night clubs, jazz clubs, museums and more. I loved our life there. I thought that we would be happy forever. I was wrong. Stephen fell in love with something other than me. He fell in love with porn.

I don't remember exactly when Stephen became addicted to pornography. I think it was a gradual thing that went unnoticed by me. He wanted more sexually. He found conforming to society's version of normal sex quite boring. I found his sudden desire to explore more sexual deviant behavior not only shocking but also terrifying. Maybe I knew and was just in denial. Whatever! The fact is that pornography and his behavior consequently destroyed our relationship. It turned Stephen into someone I didn't even recognize. It turned him into a sexually addictive jerk. I'm not saying that this will happen to all men who watch pornography, but it did to my Stephen. I could never have sex with him again. I could never let him look at me naked, touch me, kiss me or make love to me. While watching those whores on the porn sites he was mentally making love to them. He was mentally touching them and kissing them as though they were actually in the room right next to him. He spent months doing those things not only mentally to the bitches on the porn sites, but physically to the women he had invited into our bedroom behind my back. He was cheating on me.

It was two-o'clock in the morning. I turned over and Stephen wasn't in bed with me. Where the hell could this man be at two o'clock in the morning? I pulled the covers off of me and sat up on the side of the bed. I slipped my bedroom slippers on my feet and went to look for Stephen. The house was dark. All the lights were out. I saw a very dim light coming from the den. Why was Stephen in the den at this hour? I thought as I wiped my eyes with my hand that this man is crazy. I opened up the door to the den and there he was, Stephen. This was the first moment that I discovered my man's internet fueled porn addiction. He was sitting in the dark watching some sleazy porn site. There were a couple of naked ladies that looked like prostitutes engaging in sexual acts that absolutely disgusted me. When did my man become interested in this kind of shit? Who the hell was this man? I'm not into this sick shit and neither should my man be. I struggled to understand where he was coming from but I couldn't find an ounce of compassion for a man who

125

would turn away from me and seek companionship from another woman. Ladies, do you feel the same way I do? What would you do if you found out that your man was sneaking onto porn sites and watching naked girls? What would you say to him?

"Stephen!" I yelled out. "What are you doing? Why are you down here at two o'clock in the morning watching this disgusting stuff? What's the matter with you?"

Stephen was startled. He hurried up and turned the computer off.

"Nothing's wrong baby. I couldn't sleep so I decided to do something to occupy my mind. I came down here to take my mind off a lot of bullshit. I accidentally came across this website and I thought it was funny. That's all. I didn't intentionally come to this site. It was an accident. Come on. Let's go to bed. I'm tired enough to get some sleep now."

I ignored the whole incident and went to bed with Stephen. A week passed after the den incident. One Saturday afternoon I was busy doing chores around the house and Stephen was in the den doing some on-line billing on the computer, or so I thought. I wanted to see how far along he had gotten so I went to the den to check up on him. I tried to open the door to the den but it was locked. Why the hell would a man need to lock the door in order to pay a damn bill?

I knocked on the door and said, "Stephen, the door is locked. Why did you lock the door?"

He opened the door after a couple of minutes. "Come on in honey," he said innocently.

He was acting as though nothing was happening. I looked at him with a "what the hell are you doing" look on my face. His behavior was uncharacteristic of the man I fell in love with. His response was ambiguous at the most.

"What?" he asked with a clueless expression on his face. "Why are you looking at me like that?"

"I'm looking at you Stephen because you had the door locked to pay bills. I've seen you pay bills before Stephen. It's not that big of a deal. The door doesn't have to be locked."

"I'm sorry. I closed the door just to have some quiet time and the door must have locked by mistake. It's my bad."

"Whatever. Are you done?"

"Huh!" He had completely forgotten about paying the bills. "Oh, yeah. Yeah, I'm done. The bills are all paid."

I shook my head at him in disbelief and confusion at how dumb he was acting and went to prepare dinner. Later that night Stephen wanted to make love. I accommodated his wishes. He seduced me and I let him. We had already gone to bed and Stephen leaned over and kissed me passionately. I knew exactly what he wanted and I gave in. I wasn't really mad at Stephen just a little concerned about his strange behavior lately. He was locking himself up in rooms, spending time on the computer looking at porn and this new interest in internet sex. After we finished making love Stephen held me close to him.

"Honey that was fantastic," I said with total satisfaction. "It's been awhile since we've made love. My body needed that."

As I lay on his shoulder, he gently caressed me. Suddenly, the strangest words came out of his mouth. I was shocked.

"Wouldn't it be fun if we added a third person to this little party? Wouldn't it be fun if we could have a threesome?"

Think about it. Ladies, what would you say if your man suddenly asked you if he could invite another woman into your bed and if the three of you could have sex? What would your response be?

I sat up in bed and just stared at him. I thought to myself, "Who the hell was this strange man laying next to me and what did he do with my Stephen? This is not my Stephen. This man was becoming someone I didn't even recognize." He was acting compulsively and recklessly.

"Excuse me. What did you just ask me? You're going to have to repeat what you just said because I don't think I heard you right."

Stephen sat up in bed and said enthusiastically, "Before you say no, just listen for a minute."

I interrupted him and said, "Stephen your minute was up the minute you opened up your mouth. Are you out of your damn mind? Who the hell are you? What's the matter with you? Why are you acting this way? You're becoming incorrigible. Where is the man that I met over a year ago? Where is he? Who the hell are you?"

Stephen tried to convince me that adding another woman to our bed would be just what we needed to spice things up in our bedroom.

"Listen Tanya!" he pleaded. "I'm not saying that I don't love you and enjoy making love to you, because I do. That's not it. I just thought that adding another woman to the equation would really bring excitement to our relationship. It would be daring, unconventional, and completely out of our comfort zone. Don't you find that just a little bit exciting?"

I looked at him with an evil expression on my face and said sarcastically, "If you want excitement the only things you are allowed to bring into this bedroom is some whipped cream and an ice cube. There are all kinds of kinky things I could think of for us to do to spice things up in the bedroom. But, if you think for one moment that I'm going to let you bring some scanky woman into our bed then you are out of your mind. You must have fallen down and bumped your damn head. Are you crazy?"

"Will you just think about it for one minute? Why are you being so paranoid? No one wants to hurt you. I just want to improve our sex life. That's it. Will you please think about it?"

"I won't think about it for one more second. The answer is no Stephen. I don't want to hear one more damn word about it. Do you hear me?"

I layed down, turned my back to Stephen, and went to sleep. He angrily went to sleep. He was not interested in the bland normalcy of our sex life. He wanted more. He wanted lots more. Stephen didn't give up on his plan to bring a third person into our bedroom. He continued to try and pressure me into his plan. When I wouldn't give in, he became more distant. It was like he was using emotional blackmail to get me to do what he wanted me to. He barely talked to me. He wouldn't spend any time with me. He wouldn't make love to me anymore. This concerned me the most because a sexual man like Stephen needed to have sex. If he wasn't having sex with me, than who was he having sex with? As time went on he started coming home later and later. When he was home, he was locked up in the den alone visiting x-rated porn sites. I realized that I was losing my man. I tried everything I could to get Stephen interested in me again. When he actually was home with me I fixed myself up in sexy lingerie, put make-up and perfume on and fixed my hair. Stephen wasn't interested. One night I confronted him.

"Stephen, how long are you going to punish me? Just because I won't do what you want you're going to act like you can't stand me anymore? We're still a couple and I need to know if you still love me or not. If you don't we can end this right now."

"Of course I still love you, he replied sullenly like a wounded little boy. "It's just that I asked you to do something for me and I can't understand why you can't do this one thing for me. Why can't you try it just one time? What about trying to please your man? What about me? I've always done everything I can to please you. When are you going to do what I want?"

He wouldn't give up. He kept constantly badgering me to get me to do what he wanted me to. I felt total abhorrence for what he was trying to get me to do. I just couldn't see myself participating in such deviant behavior. It wasn't me. It wasn't who I was as a woman.

"Stephen, what exactly do you want me to do? What do you want me to do to save this relationship?"

"You already know exactly what I want. You know exactly what you have to do."

"Stephen I don't know if I can go through with it. I don't know if I can handle this."

"I have a way that may ease your mind. I want you to get ready tomorrow night. Put on the sexiest outfit you have. We're going out. I have a surprise for you. You trust me don't you?"

"Yes honey. I trust you and I love you. Please be with me tonight."

"Come here," he said sexily.

He took me in his arms and we made love for the first time in days. I decided that at that moment I would do anything to keep my man even if it meant bringing another woman into our bedroom to please him. Ladies, wouldn't you do whatever it took to please your man? Wouldn't you have done the same thing? In the end I abnegated my fears and decided to just give in to his wishes.

The next night I got ready for my evening out with Stephen. I had on my very low cut, very short, sexy black dress with some stiletto high heels on. My hair and makeup was perfect. I was looking hot. Stephen came home. He looked at me and smiled.

He kissed me and said, "Wow! You look fantastic. That's my sexy baby. You're not going to regret tonight. You're going to have a lot of fun. Trust me. Relax a bit. I have to get ready and then we can leave."

"Stephen, where are we going?" I asked with suspicion. "Aren't you even going to give me a hint?"

"It's a surprise baby. Trust me. You are going to love what I have in store for you tonight. I need to take a shower so we can get out of here. Don't worry your pretty little self about nothing. I got this."

He took a shower and got dressed. He was looking fine in his Italian Suit. I was proud to go out on the town with my man, but I still didn't know where we were going. Stephen was acting so mysterious. We left and headed out on our date. Stephen drove me up to a place located in a dark alley on the east side of Manhattan. I couldn't imagine what kind of place Stephen was taking me to. There were a lot of cars parked in the lot and obviously the patrons there had a lot of money. There were only luxury and expensive sports cars parked. The cheapest car there must have cost no less than fifty thousand dollars. After Stephen parked the car he helped me out of the car like a gentleman. He held my hand as he walked me closer and closer to the entrance of the club. I felt like my heart was going to stop. I couldn't breathe. I was terrified. What kind of place would be located all the way back in a dark alley?

When we walked inside to my surprise the man at the front bar knew exactly who Stephen was. Obviously Stephen had been there before. A stranger walking in off the streets would not be allowed to enter. They had tight security and plenty of bouncers to ensure the clubs privacy. You had to be known or invited by someone who was known to get in. The place was exquisite and the décor was very expensive. The walls were covered with glass and crystal chandeliers hung from the ceilings. The people walking around and those on the dance floor were all dressed elegantly in their diamond jewelry and sexy designer gowns and outfits. The lights were dimmed so much that it was almost dark in there. The place was divided into several rooms. It was like being in a brothel. Each room had its own sexy theme. The women walking around had a sexy vibe about them. There were people in each room making out. Some were actually having sex. In some rooms three people were having sex with each other. This was definitely not the place for one with a sensitive heart. It wasn't even the place for anyone with morals. It wasn't the right place for me. But, here I was. I was in a world that you only saw in the movies or on sex tapes. These places were real. For some reason they had appeared to me to be nothing more than fantasy. It was a place where there were no boundaries. There were no rules. You could be anything you wanted and do whatever you wanted and no one would tell. Everything was a secret in there to the outside world. Whatever happened in that place, stayed in there. It was the perfect place to have a ménage à trois and no one would know.

I whispered to Stephen that I didn't feel comfortable being in a place like that. I wasn't ready for an intimate encounter with a stranger. I wasn't sure I'd ever be. I never envisioned that our relationship would come to this. I told him that I wanted to go home.

"Hell no," he whispered angrily. "We just got here. Now don't back your scared ass out on me now. You promised me that you would do this. Calm the fuck down."

He told the bartender to give me a strong drink without even saying a word. They just looked at each other and Stephen nodded his head. The bartender nodded his head back. The bartender knew exactly what to do without hearing the words coming out of my man's mouth. The bartender Kareem gave me the drink and I didn't even know what was in it. I didn't care. I needed something to calm me down. I drank it down faster than I usually did. Coming to that place was my first mistake. Drinking the drink so fast was my second. I lost myself. The drink was so strong I got tipsy quickly. My head was spinning but I was feeling good. I felt like I was hallucinating. The room began to spin. I began to relax and let down my guard. Stephen and I slow danced along with a few other couples who were on the dance floor. It was very sexy and sensual. Stephen kissed me passionately and began to rub my breasts and my ass. He didn't care if people were looking or not. In fact, the more people watched the more turned on he got. I felt like I was being swept off my feet. I started to feel like I was in a dream. I didn't know whether it was the drink or the place itself that was making me feel that way. What the hell was in that drink anyway? He was taking me into a slow and secretive descent into a world of decadence and erotic behavior. He was about to change the very essence of who I was as a woman. Stephen led me slowly into one of the back rooms. As he led me off the dance floor I felt everyone staring at us. I guessed that they wanted to know who the new hot sexy woman to the club was. I was like fresh meat to them.

The lights were dimmed in the room but I could see that there was a woman lying in there. She was a very voluptuous woman. She called herself Candy. She was the kind of woman that was not only irresistible to men, but to women as well. She was mysterious, emotionally strong, yet vulnerable as well. She knew how to make a man feel like a man and a woman feel like a woman. She knew how to please. She had only panties on and no bra. She was obviously a very sexual woman and wasn't afraid to let everyone know it. She was lying on her back with her breasts up in the air for the whole world to see. Her body silhouetted as the dim strobe lights flashed across her half naked body. Stephen was turned on. I was completely abashed. My man led me into the room and introduced me to her. He knew this strange woman. Obviously they had been together before.

Stephen wanted me to take part in sexual aberrant behavior. I felt a deep sense of uneasiness and total anguish but I couldn't leave. I was too intoxicated and in total shock. Stephen slowly started to undress me as the woman watched. She seemed to be getting turned on just by him undressing me. He walked slowly over to the couch and slowly pulled her panties off. It was provocative and naughty. He layed on top of her and gently caressed her breasts as he kissed her passionately. I was taken aloof for a second. Something strange had been added to my drink. The drink that my man had given me made me utterly powerless even in my desire to stop and resist them. I was drugged and began to feel like I was in the middle of a dream that I couldn't wake up from. Despite my awareness of how wrong this seductive immoral lifestyle was, I found myself drawn into it. Part of me was drawn into it because of the drugged induced state that I was in. The other reason I was drawn into it was simple curiosity. Deep down in my sub conscience I wanted to feel what it felt like to be engaged in a threesome. I was surprised at how gentle he was being with her. He had already stopped being that soft and gentle with me and I was his woman. I was shocked at the indecency in his behavior and of my own. Stephen got off of her and slowly walked over to me. He led me over to her and laid me down next to her. She started caressing me and kissing me all over my body. I was being deliberately seduced. My man poured me a drink and slowly poured it into my mouth. He wanted to make sure I stayed in a sexy mood. Then he started to kiss Candy. As he kissed her he caressed her nipples.

The three of us took turns making love to one another. It was disgusting, sexy and erotic all at the same time. But, I couldn't stop myself. I was exhilarated. I got into it more and more. It shocked me at how little resistance I showed her. Who was I? My body relaxed and I allowed them both to take me. The excitement inside all three of us grew. We took each other to a state of total ecstasy. I reached my highest level of pleasure and my body exploded. Sometimes my man would watch as I made love with the woman. He looked at me with a feeling of accomplishment. Sometimes she would watch as my man and I made love. The entire experience was very sinful and erotic.

I don't even remember going home that night. I must have passed out. All I remember is waking up the next morning at home in my own bed. I got up to go take a shower and clean myself up. I stopped in front of the mirror and looked at my own reflection. I couldn't recognize myself anymore. Who the hell was I? What the hell was I becoming? This erratic lifestyle wasn't something I was use to. I became disgusted with myself. I was ashamed. I didn't know what to do. I ran in the bathroom and vomited. I got in the shower and scrubbed my skin so hard it turned red all over. I guess I was trying to wash the entire evening away. But, that was impossible. It was too late. I was tormented for days after that night and was having trouble sleeping at night. I had nightmares for several nights after that evening. I felt sleazy and cheap. My thoughts were full of self-hatred and I was disgusted with myself. I was ashamed of myself. I pulled away from family and friends. I didn't feel that I could talk to Stephen because he was pleased with the evening. He got exactly what he wanted. I felt alone and helpless. I thought that giving into Stephen's needs would bring him closer to me but that didn't happen. He emotionally deserted me. Even when he was home he wasn't really there. His mind was on other women and porn. He spent more and more time on internet porn sites and away from home screwing who knows. One thing I do know, he wasn't spending any time with me. He wanted to find another woman to be with. I had become a liability to him.

As time went on he became more and more of a bastard. The sporadic episodes of affection he did show me were dismal at the most. He was transforming into someone I couldn't recognize. I developed a sense of self-loathing. I was ashamed, hurt and felt desperate. I was lonely and afraid. I missed Stephen. He was pulling further and further away from me. I didn't know what to do. Then one night he finally made his way home at a decent hour. He wasn't alone though. I heard a woman's voice coming from the living room. I couldn't imagine who had come with him. Guess who he brought home to me? It was the scanky woman from the club. It was Candy. Those two actually wanted an encore performance of the other night. No one was able to slip anything into my drink this time. I wasn't drinking anything.

I was in total control of the situation and of my own body. I was no longer interested in living a life of immorality.

I looked at Stephen and said straight out, "No! Get this whore out of our house. This is not going to happen in my home or any place else anymore."

Candy came over to me and said, "Be cool bitch. Stop tripping. I just thought we could get together and have some fun. You know you want it. You wanted it the other night. You let me do things to you that even your man didn't know about. Don't try to pretend like you're better than us because I know better. You forget I know every inch of you. You're pathetic. Sitting here with this holier than thou attitude. Shit! You're not even worth it." She walked over to our bed and smiled.

She said sarcastically, "I remember this bed. A lot of sweet sexy things happened here. Right baby?" she asked Stephen.

Obviously this bitch had been physically intimate with my man in my bed before. Candy looked me up and down like I was a piece of meat and she was a starving dog.

My man was furious at my opposition to another threesome. Stephen came over to me and said, "Look. Be cool honey. No one wants to hurt you. We just want to have some fun. I know you had a good time the other night. It was the best sex we've had in years. You were hot. It could be fun like that again. Come on. Do it for your man. Don't you want to prove to me how much you love me? Come on. Don't be such a prude."

I couldn't believe I let Stephen talk me into going out to that sleazy club and behaving the way I did. What was I thinking? At that moment I realized I was better than both of them. I was a child of God. My body was a temple of the Spirit of God. How in the name of God did I get to that point? I realized that my spirit and the very essence of me had been suppressed by a man who had absolutely no respect for me at all. I meant nothing to him. Just for a moment in time I forgot who I was. I was a child of God himself. I had the Holy Spirit himself within me. He was trying to guide me and lead me to Jesus himself. The Holy Spirit of God was trying to show me that Jesus sacrificed his life for me and all the other women out there who were going through the same torment that I was. How did this happen? How did I get to the point where I forgot the power that was within me? How could I let a man lower me to this state? How could I be so weak? I can't believe I allowed myself to get caught up into Stephen's world of sex, drugs, and porn. What was I thinking? Who was I becoming? I didn't even recognize myself anymore. This was not me. I felt like I was losing myself. I couldn't do anything about the other night, but I could do something then.

At that moment I made a decision. I decided that I wasn't going to tolerate his nonsense anymore. I wasn't going to be caught up in this sick world anymore. I couldn't trust him with my life, my love or my spirit. I couldn't trust him with me. I had to take control of myself and guard my heart from being destroyed by him. I became my own woman. I found my voice and my place in God. I told Stephen to take his scanky whore and get out of my house. I told him that it was over and I never wanted to see him again.

Stephen yelled, "Who do you think you are? You don't leave me until I tell you to leave me. I own you. You're my bitch and you'll do what I say."

I put him in his place. "Stephen nobody owns me," I yelled. "I'm my own woman and I decide what happens in my life. I don't even recognize you anymore and as of now I don't want to know you. It's over Stephen. Get out of here before I call the police."

The trick from the club grabbed onto Stephen's arm and said, "Come on honey. We're wasting our time here. We don't need this bitch. She's nothing but a cunt anyway. Her pussy is not that good anyway. Shit! Let's get out of here. I know some swingers who would love to party with us tonight. Forget her."

"Yeah. You know you're right Candy," he responded with a self-righteous attitude. "I don't need this bitch". He French kissed her right in front of me and then said, "Forget you Tanya. You ain't all that. Your sex is whack anyway. You don't even know how to please a man. I don't even know why I'm wasting my time with your trifling ass. Come on baby."

He held onto the trick's arm and as they walked out a stupid grin was on her face. She was grinning because she knew that at that moment Stephen was her man. She didn't know that I didn't give a damn if Stephen was her new man. As far as I was concerned she wasn't getting much. Stephen was nothing more than a piece of garbage. I wanted to slap her but she wasn't worth it. He wasn't worth it. God required that I forgive my enemies. To please him I did. I was just glad that they were just getting out of my house and out of my life.

After I got through my anger and humiliation I realized something. That pathetic woman didn't realize that her spirit as a child of God was gone. I didn't know if she would ever find her way to Jesus but instead of judging her I prayed for her. I prayed that if she didn't find her way to Jesus he would continue to try to reach her. She needed him. She needed him to forgive her sins and grant her the gift of eternal life through the sacrifice he made by allowing himself to be die on the cross. No, I didn't judge her or hate her. I forgave her as Jesus forgives us for all of our sins and transgressions. I decided at the moment to let God and only God be her judge. It is what he wants. Through our pain and humiliation he wants us to trust him. There is something that is even more important than that. He wants us to forgive those who transgress against us. He wants us to forgive those that hurt us and betray us. He wants to be the judge of all of us.

Ladies, your salvation is more important than your pain and hatred. You are worth spending eternity serving Jesus and being a child of God. You are worth it. God loves you and no matter what your man does to hurt you God will always be your father in heaven. His love endures forever. He will never leave you or abandon you. He is not a man. He is eternal. He knows not how to betray or hurt you. In your saddest moments turn to him. Pray to him. Trust in him. He will not let you down. That inner voice that you hear is God. Trust your inner self and know that you are being guided by the Spirit of God. I had done so many things that night that I was ashamed of. Eventually I forgave myself completely. I had to in order to go on with life and survive. I didn't want to spiral down into a life of self-hatred and self-loathing. I was a better woman than that. I made a decision to become abstinent. I decided to take time to rebuild me and become the woman that I once was. I no longer hated myself or loathed myself for what I had done. I forgave myself. There are millions of women all over the world just like me. We are as one.

www.ingramcontent.com/pod-product-compliance
Lightning Source LLC
Chambersburg PA
CBHW051422280526
45785CB00003B/1124